Consulting Gold: The Roadmap to Wealth and Success & Cultivating Success in the Business Garden

By

JOSE R. JOHNSON

Table of contents:

Introduction

Unlocking Your Path to Prosperity: Embracing the Wealthy Consultant Mindset

In the huge scene of expert undertakings, hardly any ways offer the commitment of as much opportunity, adaptability, and monetary compensation as that of a specialist. However, setting out on this excursion can be much the same as exploring strange waters, full of vulnerability, challenges, and a periodic tempest. In any case, for those with the boldness to head out and the assurance to climate the difficulties, the prizes are plentiful, and the skyline is boundless.

At its center, the excursion to turning into a rich specialist starts not with the collection of abundance, but rather with an outlook — a mentality established in desire, development, and a steadfast confidence in one's capacity to make worth and impact change. An outlook sees deterrents not as unconquerable obstructions but rather as any open doors for development and learning. An outlook embraces risk, rejects smugness, and flourishes with the excitement of the unexplored world.

Embracing the rich expert mentality isn't only about making monetary progress; it is tied in with developing an all encompassing way to deal with life and work that focuses on energy, reason, and satisfaction. About perceiving genuine abundance reaches out a long ways past financial wealth and incorporates a rich embroidery of encounters, connections, and commitments to the world.

In this presentation, I will dig into the major rules that support the affluent expert mentality and investigate how you can saddle its ability to open your way to success.

Embracing Aspiration and Development

At the core of the rich expert outlook lies a persevering drive for greatness and a pledge to development. It is tied in with pushing the limits of what is conceivable, rocking the boat, and hoping against hope huge. It is tied in with declining to agree to unremarkableness and on second thought taking a stab at significance in all that you do.

Embracing aspiration implies defining bold objectives and persistently seeking after them with enthusiasm and assurance. It implies declining to let apprehension about disappointment or dismissal keep you down and on second thought embracing each mishap as a valuable chance to learn, develop, and move along.

Additionally, embracing advancement implies continually searching out groundbreaking thoughts, new methodologies, and new answers for issues. It implies being willing to consider new ideas, go ahead with well balanced plans of action, and embrace trial and error and emphasis as fundamental parts of the innovative approach.

Together, desire and advancement structure the twin motors that drive the affluent expert forward, moving them towards ever more prominent levels of accomplishment and satisfaction.

Developing Flexibility and Versatility

In the speedy universe of counseling, versatility and flexibility are not only positive qualities; they are outright necessities. The capacity to return quickly from misfortunes, adjust to evolving conditions, and flourish despite affliction separates the really effective specialist from the rest.

Developing flexibility implies fostering the psychological sturdiness and close to home grit to persist notwithstanding difficulties and misfortunes. It implies declining to be deterred by disappointment or misfortunes and on second thought seeing them as any open doors for development and learning.

Likewise, developing versatility implies being willing to embrace change, quickly take advantage of new chances, and turn course when essential. It implies perceiving that the main steady in life is change and being willing to advance and adjust to fulfill the needs of a steadily impacting world.

Together, strength and versatility structure the bedrock whereupon the well off specialist assembles their prosperity, permitting them to explore the tempestuous waters of the counseling scene with beauty, balance, and certainty.

Cultivating Coordinated effort and Association

While aspiration and advancement might drive the rich advisor forward, cooperation and association fuel their prosperity. In the hyper-associated universe of counseling, achievement is seldom accomplished in separation; it is the aftereffect of coordinated effort, collaboration, and organization with others.

Cultivating cooperation implies perceiving that you can't do it in isolation and being willing to search out and use the aptitude, experiences, and assets of others. It implies areas of strength for building, gainful associations with clients, partners, and industry companions and cooperating towards shared objectives and goals.

Also, cultivating association implies perceiving the intrinsic worth of human association and focusing on significant connections and cooperations in all parts of your life and work. It implies being available, drew in, and sympathetic in your cooperations with others and developing a feeling of having a place and local area any place you go.

Together, cooperation and association structure the social texture that ties the rich expert to their clients, partners, and industry peers, making an organization of help, motivation, and opportunity that drives them towards ever better progress and satisfaction.

The excursion to turning into a rich specialist isn't for weak willed. It requires fortitude, assurance, and an eagerness to embrace the unexplored world. In any case, so that those with the vision might own it, the prizes are vast, and the conceivable outcomes are unfathomable.

By embracing the well off specialist mentality — by developing desire and development, strength and flexibility, joint effort and association — you can open your way to flourishing and diagram a course towards a future loaded up with progress, satisfaction, and overflow.

Thus, as you leave on this excursion, I urge you to embrace the difficulties that lie ahead, quickly take advantage of the chances that current themselves, or more all, never neglect to focus on the mind blowing expected that exists in you.

Consulting Gold

Chapter 1:

Planting Seeds of Success

In the domain of business, achievement isn't just an objective; it is an excursion — an excursion set apart by endless decisions, activities, and choices that shape the direction of one's vocation and characterize the heritage they abandon. At the core of this excursion lies the idea of sowing seeds of progress — a figurative portrayal of the conscious activities and systems that people utilize to develop development, accomplish their objectives, and understand their maximum capacity.

Sowing seeds of progress starts with an outlook — a mentality established in desire, vision, and an immovable confidence in one's capacity to make worth and impact change. An outlook considers each test to be an open door, each mishap as an illustration, and each disappointment as a venturing stone on the way to significance. An outlook rejects smugness and embraces the quest for greatness in all undertakings.

At its center, sowing seeds of accomplishment is tied in with establishing the groundwork for future development and thriving. It is tied in with taking conscious, deliberate activities today that will yield profits tomorrow. Similarly as a rancher cautiously chooses and supports the seeds they plant in the dirt, so too should people in the business world develop their abilities, gifts, and connections to guarantee a plentiful gather from now on.

One of the main seeds that fruitful people plant is that of mindfulness. Mindfulness is the foundation of individual and expert development, as it empowers people to recognize their assets, shortcomings, and regions for development with clearness and genuineness. By developing mindfulness, people can use their assets for their potential benefit, alleviate their shortcomings, and pursue informed choices that line up with their objectives and values.

One more fundamental seed of accomplishment is that of objective setting. Objectives give people bearing, reason, and inspiration, filling in as signals to direct their activities and choices chasing after greatness. Whether it's accomplishing a particular achievement, arriving at a monetary objective, or having a significant effect in their industry, setting clear, noteworthy objectives engages people to zero in their energy and assets on the main thing most.

Notwithstanding mindfulness and objective setting, effective people additionally plant the seed of strength. Strength is the capacity to return quickly from misfortunes, adjust to change, and endure despite difficulty — a quality that is basic in the cutthroat universe of business. By developing flexibility, people can climate the unavoidable tempests that emerge along their excursion and arise more grounded, smarter, not entirely set in stone than any time in recent memory.

In addition, fruitful people perceive the significance of ceaseless learning and development and effectively develop the seed of interest. Interest energizes development, imagination, and flexibility, empowering people to remain on top of things in an always advancing scene. By staying liberal, curious, and responsive to novel thoughts and viewpoints, people can extend their viewpoints, challenge their suspicions, and open new open doors for development and improvement.

One more pivotal seed of progress is that of key systems administration. In the interconnected universe of business, connections are significant resources that can open entryways, encourage cooperation, and set out open doors for progression. By putting time and exertion in building and sustaining significant associations with partners, clients, guides, and industry peers, people can take advantage of an immense repository of information, backing, and assets that can move them towards their objectives.

Besides, fruitful people figure out the significance of going ahead with carefully weighed out courses of action and sow the seed of fortitude. Boldness is the readiness to step outside one's usual range of familiarity, stand up to vulnerability, and embrace the obscure — a quality that is fundamental for development and development. By thinking for even a moment to take strong, unequivocal activity in quest for their objectives, people can break liberated from the limitations of dread and uncertainty and open additional opportunities for progress.

In, sowing seeds of progress is definitely not a one-time occasion however a continuous cycle — an excursion of self-revelation, development, and change that unfurls over the long haul. By developing the seeds of mindfulness, objective setting, versatility, interest, systems administration, and boldness, people can make a strong starting point for future achievement and understand their maximum capacity in the space of business undoubtedly.

Similarly as a strong oak tree starts as a little oak seed, so too could people at any point plant the seeds of progress today that will develop into transcending accomplishments tomorrow. In this way, as you set out on your own excursion of progress, I urge you to plant the seeds of significance with aim, reason, and unfaltering assurance. The collect is standing by.

Setting the Stage

In the dynamic and cutthroat scene of the business world, achievement is much of the time decided by the moves made as well as by the establishment whereupon those activities are constructed. Making way for progress is a basic initial phase in any business try — a cycle that includes laying the preparation, characterizing the vision, and laying out the system whereupon future development and success will be constructed.

At its center, setting the stage is tied in with making the circumstances for progress to prosper. It is tied in with explaining targets, adjusting assets, and laying out a reasonable bearing that directs the activities and choices of all partners included. Whether sending off another endeavor, entering another market, or chasing after an essential drive, setting the stage really can mean the contrast among progress and disappointment.

One of the most important phases in making way for progress is characterizing the vision and mission of the business. The vision expresses the drawn out objectives and goals of the association, giving an unmistakable image of what achievement resembles and motivating partners to energize behind a typical reason. The mission, then again, frames the basic beliefs, standards, and targets that guide the everyday tasks of the business, filling in as a guide for direction and vital preparation.

A convincing vision and mission move certainty and responsibility among representatives as well as draw in clients, financial backers, and accomplices who share in the association's qualities and desires. By articulating a reasonable and convincing vision and mission, organizations can make way for progress by adjusting partners around a typical reason and heading that directs their activities and choices.

As well as characterizing the vision and mission, making way for progress likewise includes directing an intensive examination of the business climate and distinguishing key open doors and difficulties. This cycle, known as a SWOT investigation (Qualities, Shortcomings, Open doors, Dangers), permits organizations to survey their interior capacities and outside market elements, distinguish areas of upper hand, and foster systems to profit by open doors and moderate dangers.

By leading an extensive SWOT examination, organizations can acquire important bits of knowledge into their cutthroat position, market elements, and industry patterns, empowering them to go with informed choices and designate assets really. Whether it's recognizing undiscovered market sections, tending to cutthroat dangers, or utilizing arising innovations, an intensive comprehension of the business climate is fundamental for making way for progress.

Besides, making way for progress expects organizations to characterize clear objectives and targets that give a guide to activity and measure progress towards accomplishing the vision and mission. Objectives ought to be explicit, quantifiable, reachable, significant, and time-bound (Shrewd), giving an unmistakable system to direction and responsibility.

Whether it's rising piece of the pie, venturing into new regions, or working on functional effectiveness, defining clear objectives and goals helps center endeavors and assets around exercises that drive significant advancement towards the association's drawn out vision and mission. By adjusting objectives to the more extensive key needs of the business, associations can make way for progress by making a common feeling of direction and course that directs the activities and choices, everything being equal.

Besides, making way for progress includes making a culture of development, cooperation, and constant improvement that enables workers to release their maximum capacity and drive significant change. A culture that supports trial and error, embraces variety of thought, and rewards inventiveness encourages a climate where groundbreaking thoughts can thrive, forward leaps can happen, and hindrances to progress can be survived.

By putting resources into worker improvement, encouraging a feeling of coordinated effort, and giving open doors to development and progression, associations can develop a culture of greatness that draws in top ability, moves advancement, and drives reasonable achievement. A solid hierarchical culture improves representative commitment and maintenance as well as fills in as a strong differentiator that separates organizations in the commercial center.

As well as making a culture of development and coordinated effort, making way for progress likewise includes laying out vigorous frameworks and cycles that empower productive and successful execution of key drives. From project the board and execution estimation to gamble with the executives and independent direction, obvious frameworks and cycles give the construction and backing expected to make an interpretation of vision right into it and drive results.

By executing best works on, utilizing innovation, and ceaselessly advancing activities, organizations can smooth out work processes, further develop efficiency, and improve deftness, guaranteeing that they stay receptive to changing business sector elements and cutthroat tensions. Whether it's smoothing out store network activities, upgrading client assistance processes, or executing lean assembling standards, putting resources into frameworks and cycles that help key targets is fundamental for making way for progress.

Additionally, making way for progress expects organizations to lay areas of strength for out and associations with key partners, including clients, providers, financial backers, and administrative specialists. Building trust, encouraging open correspondence, and adjusting interests are fundamental for developing commonly advantageous connections that drive long haul esteem creation and economical development.

Whether it's fashioning key partnerships, participating in joint endeavors, or teaming up with industry affiliations, organizations must proactively search out amazing chances to work together and co-make esteem with key partners. By building solid connections and associations, associations can get to new business sectors, extend their scope, and open new open doors for development and advancement.

In, making way for progress is a multi-layered process that includes characterizing the vision and mission, directing an exhaustive examination of the business climate, defining clear objectives and goals, making a culture of development and joint effort, laying out powerful frameworks and cycles, and building solid connections and organizations with key partners. By taking purposeful, deliberate activities to lay the basis for future achievement, organizations can make a strong groundwork whereupon to construct and accomplish their drawn out objectives and goals.

Similarly as a very much fabricated stage gives the establishment to a critical presentation, so too does setting the stage really lay the basis for progress in the business world. In this way, as you set out on your own excursion of progress, I urge you to get some margin to set the stage appropriately, guaranteeing that you have a strong groundwork whereupon to construct and accomplish your fantasies.

Establishments for Counseling Riches

In the present quick moving and interconnected business scene, the counseling business assumes a pivotal part in driving development, taking care of complicated issues, and driving hierarchical change. As organizations endeavor to remain on the ball and explore an undeniably serious and unsure climate, the interest for counseling administrations keeps on developing, introducing worthwhile open doors for advisors to flourish and succeed. In any case, outcome in the counseling business isn't ensured and requires a strong groundwork based on key standards, techniques, and abilities that empower specialists to convey extraordinary worth and make practical progress.

In this far reaching guide, we will investigate the establishments for counseling abundance in the cutting edge business world, covering fundamental subjects, for example, understanding the counseling scene, creating mastery and specialization, constructing areas of strength for a brand, developing vital connections, and conveying unmistakable outcomes for clients. By dominating these central standards and procedures, specialists can situate themselves for long haul achievement and open their maximum capacity in the serious counseling industry.

Understanding the Counseling Scene

The counseling scene is different and multi-layered, enveloping many businesses, areas, and strengths. From the board counseling and methodology improvement to innovation execution and hierarchical change, specialists assume a fundamental part in assisting organizations with handling their most squeezing difficulties and jump all over new chances for development and advancement.

To prevail in the counseling business, it is fundamental to have a profound comprehension of the different areas, enterprises, and markets in which you work. This incorporates keeping up to date with industry patterns, market elements, and arising innovations that might affect your clients' organizations and illuminate your counseling approach.

Also, advisors should have the option to adjust to the developing requirements and inclinations of their clients and designer their administrations to address explicit difficulties and open doors. This requires adaptability, dexterity, and a readiness to embrace change and development to convey esteem added arrangements that drive quantifiable outcomes for clients.

Creating Aptitude and Specialization

In a profoundly serious counseling business sector, mastery and specialization are key differentiators that put experts aside from their friends and empower them to order higher expenses and draw in top-level clients. By growing profound space information and skill in a particular industry, area, or utilitarian region, specialists can situate themselves as believed guides and well-informed authorities who can give significant bits of knowledge, exhortation, and answers for clients.

Specialization permits advisors to zero in their endeavors and assets on regions where they can convey the most worth and have the best effect. Whether it's top to bottom information on a specific industry vertical, skill in a particular innovation stage, or dominance of a particular system or approach, specialization empowers experts to separate themselves from the opposition and cut out an extraordinary specialty on the lookout.

Besides, creating mastery and specialization requires a pledge to consistent learning and expert turn of events. This incorporates keeping up to date with industry patterns, best practices, and arising innovations, as well as seeking after cutting edge confirmations, preparing programs, and instructive open doors that improve your abilities and capacities as an expert.

Creating Serious areas of courage for a Brand

In the present computerized age, individual marking has turned into a fundamental part of progress in the counseling business. A solid individual brand assists specialists with laying out believability, perceivability, and authority in their picked field, situating them as figured pioneers and industry specialists who can give significant experiences, counsel, and answers for clients.

Building areas of strength for a brand begins with characterizing your remarkable incentive and distinguishing what separates you from different experts on the lookout. This might incorporate your ability, experience, history of progress, or extraordinary point of view on industry patterns and issues.

Whenever you have recognized your exceptional offer, it's critical to impart it actually through your on the web and disconnected presence. This incorporates upgrading your LinkedIn profile and other virtual entertainment channels, making excellent substance, for example, blog entries, articles, and whitepapers, and partaking in industry occasions, meetings, and systems administration open doors where you can grandstand your ability and associate with likely clients and accomplices.

Besides, building major areas of strength for a brand requires consistency, credibility, and straightforwardness in your collaborations with clients, partners, and industry peers. By reliably conveying esteem, showing uprightness, and building entrust with your crowd, you can develop serious areas of strength for a brand that resounds with clients and assists you with hanging out in a jam-packed commercial center.

Developing Key Connections

In the counseling business, connections mean the world. Developing key associations with clients, partners, and industry peers is fundamental for progress, as it empowers advisors to get to new open doors, extend their organization, and open new wellsprings of significant worth and development.

Building solid associations with clients starts with figuring out their requirements, targets, and difficulties and exhibiting a veritable interest in assisting them with accomplishing their objectives. This requires undivided attention, sympathy, and a readiness to exceed everyone's expectations to convey extraordinary worth and administration to clients.

Besides, developing vital associations with partners and industry companions can offer significant help, mentorship, and joint effort potential open doors that can improve your abilities and capacities as an expert. By partaking in industry affiliations, organizing occasions, and expert improvement programs, you can associate with similar experts, trade thoughts and best practices, and keep up to date with industry patterns and advancements.

Moreover, essential connections can likewise give admittance to new clients, reference open doors, and organization prospects that can fuel your development and extension as a specialist. By putting time and exertion in building and sustaining associations with key partners, you can make areas of strength for an organization that enables you to accomplish your objectives and goals in the counseling business.

Conveying Substantial Outcomes for Clients

Eventually, progress in the counseling business depends on the capacity to convey substantial outcomes and quantifiable incentive for clients. Whether it's rising income, lessening costs, working on functional productivity, or driving development, experts should show a history of progress and a promise to conveying results that line up with clients' essential goals and business needs.

Conveying substantial outcomes for clients requires a mix of specialized mastery, logical abilities, and key reasoning, as well as successful correspondence, cooperation, and venture the executives capacities. Experts should have the option to recognize key open doors for development, foster information driven proposals, and execute pragmatic arrangements that drive quantifiable outcomes and create a positive profit from venture for clients.

Besides, experts should likewise have the option to successfully impart their discoveries, proposals, and bits of knowledge to clients in an unmistakable, convincing, and noteworthy way. This remembers introducing complex data for an edible configuration, building agreement among key partners, and offering progressing help and direction all through the execution cycle to guarantee a good outcome.

By reliably conveying unmistakable outcomes and quantifiable incentive for clients, specialists can construct a standing for greatness and procure the trust and unwaveringness of their clients, making ready for long haul achievement and thriving in the counseling business

In, creating financial stability in the counseling business requires a strong groundwork based on key standards, methodologies, and abilities that empower experts to convey outstanding worth and make manageable progress. By understanding the counseling scene, creating mastery and specialization, fabricating major areas of strength for a brand, developing key connections, and conveying substantial outcomes for clients, experts can situate themselves for long haul achievement and open their maximum capacity in the serious counseling industry.

Similarly as a very much fabricated establishment gives security and backing to a high rise, so too helps out establishment give the preparation to progress and success in the counseling business. Thus, as you set out on your excursion to counseling abundance, I urge you to zero in on dominating these primary standards and methodologies and applying them reliably in your training. With devotion, diligence, and a pledge to greatness, you can accomplish your objectives and desires and fabricate a fruitful and remunerating profession in the counseling business.

Chapter 2:

Unleashing Your Consulting Potential

In the steadily developing scene of business and industry, counseling has arisen as a dynamic and compelling calling, offering people the valuable chance to use their mastery, imagination, and vital reasoning to drive significant change and have a constructive outcome on associations of all sizes and ventures. Notwithstanding, understanding your maximum capacity as a specialist requires something other than specialized skill and industry information — it requires an outlook of development, cooperation, and ceaseless improvement that engages you to adjust, develop, and flourish in a consistently impacting world.

In this aide, we will investigate systems and methods for releasing your counseling potential, assisting you with boosting your effect, accomplish your objectives, and understand your maximum capacity as an expert.

Embracing the Advisor Attitude

At the core of releasing your counseling potential is embracing the expert mentality — an outlook established in interest, imagination, and a tenacious drive for greatness. An outlook considers difficulties to be open doors, requirements as impetuses for development, and disappointment as a venturing stone on the way to progress. By embracing this mentality, you can open your natural potential and outfit your exceptional assets and capacities to have a significant effect in the counseling business.

One of the critical parts of the specialist outlook is a promise to long lasting learning and expert turn of events. In a quickly impacting world, remaining on the ball requires a readiness to persistently extend your insight, abilities, and capacities through continuous schooling, preparing, and experience. Whether it's dominating new advancements, finding out about arising industry drifts, or leveling up your administration and correspondence abilities, putting resources into your own and proficient development is fundamental for releasing your counseling potential.

In addition, the specialist outlook likewise stresses the significance of coordinated effort and collaboration in accomplishing shared objectives and goals. In the present interconnected world, achievement is seldom accomplished in confinement — it requires the aggregate exertion and skill of different people cooperating towards a typical reason. By encouraging a culture of cooperation, receptiveness, and common regard, you can use the aggregate insight and imagination of your group to take care of perplexing issues, drive development, and accomplish unprecedented outcomes.

Recognizing Your Remarkable Offer

One more fundamental part of releasing your counseling potential is recognizing and utilizing your remarkable offer — the blend of abilities, encounters, and skill that separates you from different specialists on the lookout. Your remarkable offer recognizes you from your rivals and positions you as the go-to master in your field.

To distinguish your interesting incentive, begin by considering your center assets, interests, and subject matters. What are you exceptionally qualified to offer clients? What issues do you succeed at settling? What separates you from different advisors in your industry? By responding to these inquiries genuinely and nicely, you can start to reveal your novel incentive and distinguish the regions where you can increase the value of your clients.

Whenever you have recognized your one of a kind incentive, it's essential to impart it successfully to your ideal interest group. This incorporates refreshing your resume, LinkedIn profile, and other expert materials to feature your critical assets and achievements, as well as fostering a convincing short presentation that compactly imparts what your identity is, what you do, and why clients ought to pick you over the opposition.

Also, displaying your special offer through figured administration and content advertising can assist you with laying out believability, perceivability, and authority in your picked field. Whether it's composing articles, talking at gatherings, or facilitating online classes, offering your experiences and mastery to others exhibits your ability as well as draws in potential clients who are looking for your particular abilities and capacities.

Fostering a Development Outlook

As well as embracing the specialist outlook and recognizing your remarkable incentive, releasing your counseling potential likewise requires fostering a development mentality — a conviction that your capacities and insight can be created through devotion and difficult work. A development outlook engages you to embrace difficulties, persevere notwithstanding mishaps, and view disappointment as a chance for development and learning.

One of the vital standards of a development outlook is the conviction that ability and knowledge are not fixed qualities but rather can be created and worked on over the long haul through exertion and determination. By embracing this conviction, you can beat self-restricting convictions and release your maximum capacity as a specialist, driving yourself to ceaselessly learn, develop, and develop in your vocation.

Besides, a development outlook likewise underscores the significance of embracing input and analysis as any open doors for development and improvement. Rather than survey criticism as an individual assault or an impression of your capacities, see it as important information that can assist you with distinguishing vulnerable sides, defeat shortcomings, and refine your abilities and capacities. By searching out input from clients, partners, and coaches, you can acquire significant experiences into regions for development and find proactive ways to address them, eventually improving your viability and effect as an expert.

Making a move and Embracing Hazard

At long last, releasing your counseling potential requires making a move and embracing risk — an eagerness to step outside your usual range of familiarity, take on new difficulties, and seek after valuable open doors that push you to develop and advance as a specialist. It's tied in with being proactive, clever, and strong despite vulnerability, and immediately jumping all over the opportunity to have a beneficial outcome on the planet.

Making a move requires mental fortitude, certainty, and an eagerness to embrace disappointment as a characteristic piece of the educational experience. It's tied in with pushing past your feelings of trepidation and uncertainties and taking strong, unequivocal activity in quest for your objectives and goals. Whether it's starting a new counseling work on, chasing after a difficult task, or testing out a strong plan to a client, making a move is fundamental for releasing your counseling potential and accomplishing your maximum capacity as an expert.

Besides, embracing risk is fundamental for releasing your counseling potential, as it permits you to break liberated from the requirements of dread and vulnerability and open new open doors for development and advancement. Rather than leaving nothing to chance and adhering to business as usual, proceed with carefully thought out plans of action and seek after intense thoughts that can possibly change your profession and your life. By embracing risk and venturing outside your usual range of familiarity, you can release your maximum capacity as a specialist and have an enduring effect on the planet.

Releasing your counseling potential requires a mix of outlook, abilities, and activities that engage you to boost your effect and progress in the counseling business. By embracing the expert outlook, distinguishing your special offer, fostering a development mentality, and making a move and embracing risk, you can release your maximum capacity as a specialist and accomplish your objectives and goals in the serious and consistently impacting universe of counseling.

Thus, as you set out on your excursion to releasing your counseling potential, make sure to embrace the difficulties, quickly jump all over the chances, and believe constantly in your capacity to have a significant effect on the planet. With devotion, tirelessness, and a promise to ceaseless development and improvement, you can open your maximum capacity as a specialist and make progress beyond anything you could ever imagine.

Making way for Abundance

Chasing after monetary achievement and success, setting the stage is essential — it lays the basis, lays out the structure, and makes the circumstances for abundance to thrive. Whether you're endeavoring to construct a savings for retirement, accomplish monetary freedom, or make generational abundance for your family, setting the stage really is fundamental for accomplishing your drawn out monetary objectives. In this far reaching guide, we will investigate methodologies and procedures for making way for riches, covering key standards like monetary preparation, venture the board, risk the executives, and abundance safeguarding. By dominating these primary ideas and carrying out them in your monetary methodology, you can make a strong starting point for long haul abundance gathering and monetary security.

Grasping Monetary Preparation

At the core of making way for abundance is monetary preparation — a far reaching process that includes defining objectives, surveying assets, and creating procedures to make monetary progress. Monetary arranging envelops a large number of regions, including planning, saving, effective financial planning, retirement arranging, domain arranging, and hazard the board, and fills in as a guide for accomplishing your monetary targets.

One of the most important phases in monetary arranging is setting clear, noteworthy objectives that line up with your qualities, needs, and yearnings. Whether it's purchasing a home, putting something aside for your kids' schooling, or building a retirement savings, characterizing your monetary objectives gives guidance and inspiration for your monetary excursion and assists you with focusing on your assets and endeavors as needs be.

Whenever you have characterized your objectives, the subsequent stage is to evaluate what is happening and distinguish any holes or regions for development. This incorporates assessing your pay, costs, resources, liabilities, and income to acquire an extensive comprehension of your monetary wellbeing and recognize potential open doors for improvement and development.

Additionally, monetary arranging likewise includes creating methodologies to accomplish your objectives and alleviate gambles en route. This might incorporate making a financial plan to oversee costs, laying out a secret stash to cover startling costs, and differentiating your venture portfolio to oversee risk and expand returns.

Venture The board

One more key part of making way for abundance is venture the board — the most common way of allotting money to various resource classes and speculation vehicles fully intent on accomplishing long haul development and monetary security. Powerful venture the board requires a careful comprehension of speculation standards, market elements, and chance administration techniques, as well as a trained way to deal with portfolio development and the executives.

One of the basic standards of venture the board is resource designation — the most common way of splitting your speculation portfolio between various resource classes, like stocks, bonds, land, and elective speculations, to accomplish an equilibrium between chance and return that lines up with your venture targets and hazard resistance. By broadening your portfolio across various resource classes, you can decrease the general gamble of your speculation portfolio and work on its flexibility to advertise unpredictability and financial vulnerability.

In addition, powerful speculation the executives likewise includes choosing excellent venture vehicles and techniques that line up with your venture goals, time skyline, and hazard resistance. Whether you like to put resources into individual stocks, shared reserves, trade exchanged reserves (ETFs), or elective ventures, for example, confidential value or land, it means a lot to direct careful exploration and a reasonable level of effort to guarantee that your speculation choices are educated, key, and lined up with your drawn out monetary objectives.

Risk The board

Notwithstanding venture the executives, making way for abundance additionally requires successful gamble the board — the method involved with distinguishing, surveying, and relieving potential dangers that might compromise your monetary security and solidness. Risk the executives incorporates a great many regions, including speculation risk, market risk, credit risk, liquidity risk, expansion chance, and life span risk, and includes creating systems to limit the effect of these dangers on your monetary prosperity.

One of the best systems for risk the board is enhancement — the act of spreading your ventures across various resource classes, businesses, and geographic areas to diminish the effect of any single speculation or occasion on your general portfolio. By broadening your ventures, you can limit the gamble of misfortune and instability and further develop the general gamble changed return of your speculation portfolio.

In addition, viable gamble the board likewise includes carrying out suitable protection inclusion to safeguard against unexpected occasions and crises, like medical coverage, life coverage, handicap protection, and long haul care protection. Protection gives a wellbeing net that can assist with relieving the monetary effect of mishaps, diseases, and other unforeseen occasions, permitting you to keep up with your monetary security and dependability notwithstanding misfortune.

Abundance Protection

At last, making way for abundance likewise includes abundance conservation — the most common way of safeguarding and developing your abundance after some time to guarantee long haul monetary security and solidness. Abundance conservation incorporates many procedures and methods, including charge arranging, bequest arranging, resource security, and inheritance arranging, and includes finding a way proactive ways to protect your resources and limit the effect of duties and different costs on your riches.

One of the best systems for abundance safeguarding is charge arranging — the method involved with limiting your assessment responsibility and amplifying your after-assessment forms through essential expense saving procedures and strategies. This might incorporate exploiting charge conceded retirement accounts, for example, 401(k)s and IRAs, collecting charge misfortunes to balance capital additions, and decisively timing the offer of resources for limit charge outcomes.

Besides, successful abundance safeguarding additionally includes home preparation — the method involved with orchestrating your undertakings and resources for guarantee that your desires are completed and your friends and family are accommodated after your passing. This might incorporate making a will, laying out trusts, assigning recipients, and fostering an arrangement for moving abundance to people in the future in a duty proficient way.

Moreover, resource security is one more significant part of abundance conservation, particularly in the present belligerent society. Resource assurance includes carrying out legitimate and monetary systems to protect your resources from expected loan bosses, claims, and different liabilities, subsequently shielding your abundance and safeguarding your monetary security and dependability.

Making way for abundance requires a far reaching approach that incorporates monetary preparation, speculation the board, risk the executives, and abundance protection. By dominating these fundamental ideas and executing them successfully in your monetary procedure, you can make a strong starting point for long haul abundance collection and monetary security. Thus, as you set out on your excursion to monetary achievement and success, make sure to focus on making way for riches, and make proactive moves to lay the preparation for a splendid and prosperous future.

Amplifying Your Procuring Potential

In the present quickly evolving economy, the capacity to amplify your procuring potential is fundamental for making monetary progress and creating financial stability. Whether you're expecting to expand your pay, advance in your vocation, go into business, or put resources into rewarding open doors, boosting your procuring potential requires a blend of vital preparation, expertise improvement, and proactive activity. In this complete aide, we will investigate demonstrated systems and procedures for augmenting your acquiring potential, covering key regions like professional success, business venture, automated revenue, speculation methodologies, and monetary preparation. By carrying out these techniques really, you can open new open doors, speed up your pay development, and accomplish your monetary objectives.

Professional success

One of the most immediate methods for augmenting your acquiring potential is through professional success — ascending the company pecking order, procuring advancements, and expanding your acquiring power inside your picked field or industry. Professional success requires a blend of difficult work, devotion, and vital preparation, as well as a pledge to consistent learning and expert turn of events.

One system for propelling your vocation and amplifying your procuring potential is to seek after extra schooling and preparing that improves your abilities, capabilities, and attractiveness in the gig market. This might incorporate acquiring postgraduate educations, proficient certificates, or concentrated accreditations that show your aptitude and ability in your field and position you for more lucrative jobs and valuable open doors.

Besides, building serious areas of strength for an organization and developing associations with guides, backers, and industry companions can likewise upgrade your profession prospects and entryways to new open doors for headway. Organizing permits you to associate with compelling people who can give direction, backing, and vocation open doors, as well as admittance to important assets and data that can assist you with prevailing in your profession.

Moreover, taking on positions of authority, chipping in for testing projects, and showing a history of progress and accomplishment in your ongoing job can likewise situate you for headway and increment your procuring potential. By displaying your initiative capacities, critical thinking abilities, and capacity to drive results, you can make yourself vital to your association and stand apart as a top entertainer who merits acknowledgment and prizes.

Business

One more impressive method for expanding your procuring potential is through business — going into business, fabricating an effective endeavor, and creating different floods of pay that can fundamentally support your acquiring power and monetary freedom. Business offers unmatched open doors for abundance creation and monetary achievement, however it likewise requires an elevated degree of responsibility, risk resistance, and innovative soul.

One procedure for amplifying your acquiring potential through business venture is to recognize neglected needs, undiscovered business sectors, or arising patterns and foster creative items or administrations that address these open doors. By recognizing a specialty market or underserved client portion and making remarkable incentives that reverberate with their requirements and inclinations, you can cut out a productive business opportunity that creates significant income and benefits.

Besides, utilizing innovation and computerized stages can likewise assist you with expanding your procuring potential as a business person by contacting a more extensive crowd, scaling your business activities, and mechanizing dull errands. Whether it's selling items web based, offering computerized courses or counseling administrations, or sending off a product as-a-administration (SaaS) stage, innovation can engage you to make versatile, high-development organizations that create recurring, automated revenue and independence from the rat race.

Furthermore, building areas of strength for an and online presence can likewise upgrade your procuring potential as a business visionary by drawing in clients, building trust, and separating your business from rivals. By putting resources into promoting, marking, and client experience, you can lay down a good foundation for yourself as a believable, respectable expert in your specialty and order premium costs for your items or administrations, in this manner boosting your procuring potential and benefit.

Recurring, automated revenue

Notwithstanding dynamic pay from business or business, automated revenue is one more remarkable method for augmenting your procuring potential and accomplish independence from the rat race. Automated revenue is pay that is procured with insignificant exertion or progressing work, like rental pay from land speculations, profits from stocks and securities, sovereignties from protected innovation, or partner commissions from internet advertising.

One system for creating automated revenue and expanding your acquiring potential is to put resources into pay delivering resources that produce repeating income streams after some time. This might remember financial planning for investment properties, profit paying stocks, high return bonds, or pay producing organizations that give steady income and long haul capital appreciation.

Additionally, utilizing the force of compounding can likewise assist you with expanding your procuring possible through recurring, automated revenue by reinvesting your income and permitting them to develop dramatically over the long haul. By reinvesting profits, premium, or rental pay once again into your speculations, you can speed up the development of your portfolio and increment your recurring source of income, subsequently amplifying your long haul procuring potential and monetary security.

Moreover, making advanced resources, for example, digital books, online courses, or programming items can likewise create automated revenue by giving important substance or administrations to clients on autopilot. By utilizing advanced stages and robotization apparatuses, you can make automated sources of income that create income day in and day out, permitting you to bring in cash while you rest and amplify your bringing in potential without exchanging time for cash.

Venture Procedures

One more key technique for expanding your acquiring potential is to foster sound speculation methodologies that create alluring returns while limiting gamble and unpredictability. Viable venture systems require an exhaustive comprehension of speculation standards, market elements, and hazard the executives strategies, as well as a trained way to deal with portfolio development and the board.

One procedure for boosting your procuring potential through ventures is to embrace a long haul, purchase and-hold approach that spotlights on putting resources into top notch resources with solid basics and development possibilities. By putting resources into broadened arrangement of stocks, securities, land, and elective speculations, you can create financial wellbeing consistently after some time and accomplish your drawn out monetary objectives while limiting the effect of momentary market changes and instability.

In addition, exploiting charge effective venture methodologies can likewise assist you with amplifying your procuring potential by lessening your duty risk and boosting your after-assessment forms. This might remember effective money management for charge advantaged retirement accounts, for example, 401(k)s and IRAs, gathering charge misfortunes to counterbalance capital additions, and decisively timing the offer of resources for limit charge results.

Furthermore, consolidating elective speculations like confidential value, funding, or mutual funds into your venture portfolio can likewise assist you with boosting your procuring potential by giving admittance to extraordinary venture amazing open doors and possibly more significant yields than conventional resource classes. In any case, elective ventures likewise accompany higher dangers and expenses, so it's vital to lead careful expected level of effort and talk with a monetary counsel prior to putting resources into these resource classes.

Monetary Preparation

At last, boosting your procuring potential requires compelling monetary preparation — a thorough interaction that includes laying out objectives, evaluating assets, and creating techniques to make monetary progress. Monetary arranging envelops a large number of regions, including planning, saving, financial planning, retirement arranging, domain arranging, and chance administration, and fills in as a guide for accomplishing your monetary targets.

One system for boosting your procuring potential through monetary arranging is to lay out clear, noteworthy objectives that line up with your qualities, needs, and goals. Whether it's purchasing a home, putting something aside for your kids' schooling, or building a retirement savings, characterizing your monetary objectives gives guidance and inspiration for your monetary excursion and assists you with focusing on your assets and endeavors likewise.

Besides, fostering a financial plan and spending plan can likewise assist you with boosting your procuring potential by guaranteeing that you live inside your means, keep away from pointless costs, and dispense your assets decisively to accomplish your monetary objectives. By following your pay and costs, recognizing regions for advancement, and coming to informed conclusions about your ways of managing money, you can enhance your income and increment your reserve funds rate, accordingly amplifying your procuring possible over the long haul.

Furthermore, integrating charge effective systems into your monetary arrangement can likewise assist you with amplifying your procuring potential by lessening your duty responsibility and expanding your after-government forms. This might incorporate exploiting charge advantaged retirement accounts, for example, 401(k)s and IRAs, streamlining your speculation portfolio for charge proficiency, and decisively timing the acknowledgment of capital additions and misfortunes to limit charge outcomes.

Boosting your procuring potential requires a mix of vital preparation, expertise improvement, and proactive activity across numerous areas, including professional success, business, automated revenue, speculation systems, and monetary preparation. By executing these systems actually, you can open new open doors, speed up your pay development, and accomplish your monetary objectives, at last augmenting your acquiring potential and creating long haul financial stability and monetary security.

Along these lines, as you set out on your excursion to amplify your procuring potential, make sure to focus on constant acquiring and expertise improvement, quickly jump all over chances for development and headway, and find proactive ways to fabricate different floods of pay and enhance your monetary assets. With devotion, diligence, and a promise to greatness, you can open your full procuring potential and make monetary progress beyond anything you could ever imagine.

Chapter 3:

The Million-Dollar Mindset

In the mission for monetary achievement and overflow, mentality assumes an essential part. The manner in which we think, see, and move toward valuable open doors and provokes can fundamentally affect our capacity to accomplish our objectives and understand our fantasies. The million-dollar outlook isn't just about abundance collection; it's tied in with embracing a mentality of overflow, probability, and flexibility that enables us to release our maximum capacity and make the existence we want. In this aide, we will investigate the vital standards and procedures of the million-dollar mentality, and how you can develop it to make progress in all aspects of your life.

Faith in Overflow

At the center of the million-dollar outlook is a faith in overflow — a steady conviction that there is a very sizable amount of riches, opportunity, and accomplishment to go around. Rather than working from a shortage mindset, which is portrayed by dread, rivalry, and limit, those with 1,000,000 dollar mentality embrace overflow and consider the world to be a position of endless potential outcomes and open doors.

Trusting in overflow permits us to move toward existence with hopefulness, certainty, and transparency, realizing that there are vast opportunities for development, extension, and flourishing. Rather than review accomplishment as a lose situation where one individual's benefit is someone else's misfortune, we view accomplishment as something that can be shared and celebrated by all.

In addition, having confidence in overflow engages us to face striking challenges, seek after aggressive objectives, and think ambitiously unafraid of disappointment or shortage. It liberates us from the imperatives of self-uncertainty and limit and empowers us to take advantage of our maximum capacity and imagination to make the existence of our fantasies.

Development Mentality

One more key rule of the million-dollar outlook is the reception of a development mentality — a conviction that our capacities and insight can be created through devotion, exertion, and constancy. Rather than review difficulties as unfavorable hindrances, those with a development mentality consider them to be open doors for learning, development, and improvement.

A development mentality empowers us to embrace disappointment as a characteristic piece of the educational experience and to involve mishaps as any open doors for reflection, change, and course remedy. Rather than surrendering when confronted with affliction, we persist, adjust, and keep on pushing forward, realizing that each mishap carries us one bit nearer to progress.

Besides, a development mentality engages us to develop versatility, coarseness, and assurance — the characteristics that are fundamental for making progress notwithstanding snags and misfortune. It permits us to return from mishaps more grounded not set in stone than any time in recent memory, realizing that each challenge we beat makes us stronger and clever.

Embracing An open door

The million-dollar mentality is portrayed by a readiness to embrace an open door and jump all over the opportunity when it emerges. Rather than sitting tight for chances to come to us, we effectively search them out and exploit them when they introduce themselves.

This proactive way to deal with opportunity permits us to make our own karma and to assume command over our fate, instead of being helpless before outside conditions. It expects us to be ready, mindful, and liberal, prepared to perceive and jump all over chances at whatever point they emerge.

Also, embracing opportunity expects us to step beyond our usual ranges of familiarity and to face challenges in quest for our objectives and goals. It requires fortitude, drive, and an eagerness to embrace vulnerability and equivocalness, realizing that the best rewards frequently come from proceeding with carefully thought out plans of action and wandering into the unexplored world.

Industriousness and Flexibility

Industriousness and flexibility are two of the main characteristics of the million-dollar mentality. Despite snags, mishaps, and difficulties, those with 1,000,000 dollar mentality won't surrender or be prevented from their objectives. All things being equal, they endure, persist, and keep on pushing forward, regardless of how troublesome the excursion might be.

Determination is the fuel that drives us forward chasing after our fantasies. It empowers us to keep on track and focused on our objectives, in any event, when confronted with apparently outlandish impediments or mishaps. It requires assurance, discipline, and a never-surrender disposition, realizing that achievement is in many cases not far off for the people who will continue to push forward.

Versatility is the capacity to quickly return from disappointment, affliction, and difficulties more grounded not entirely settled than any other time in recent memory. It permits us to gain from our mix-ups, develop from our encounters, and rise up out of difficulties with freshly discovered strength and insight. Flexibility empowers us to transform misfortunes into potential open doors, deterrents into venturing stones, and difficulty into win.

Appreciation and Liberality

At long last, the million-dollar mentality is portrayed by a disposition of appreciation and liberality. Rather than zeroing in exclusively on what we need or what we need, those with 1,000,000 dollar mentality appreciate and praise the overflow that as of now exists in their lives.

Appreciation permits us to develop a feeling of overflow and satisfaction, even notwithstanding difficulties or mishaps. It empowers us to perceive and value the endowments, open doors, and gifts that we have been given, and to move toward existence with lowliness, beauty, and appreciation.

Besides, liberality is the normal outgrowth of appreciation — it is the demonstration of offering in return and imparting our endowments to other people. Liberality empowers us to have a beneficial outcome in the existences of others, to add to everyone's benefit, and to make a gradually expanding influence of benevolence, empathy, and generosity on the planet.

By developing a mentality of appreciation and liberality, we improve our own lives as well as add to the prosperity and joy of others, making a temperate pattern of overflow and flourishing that benefits every one of us.

The million-dollar outlook isn't just about abundance collection — it's tied in with taking on a mentality of overflow, probability, and versatility that enables us to release our maximum capacity and make the existence we want. By trusting in overflow, embracing a valuable open door, developing a development outlook, and showing perseverance, versatility, appreciation, and liberality, we can expand our procuring potential and make progress in all parts of our lives.

Thus, as you set out on your excursion to develop the million-dollar attitude, make sure to embrace overflow, take advantage of chances, persist notwithstanding difficulties, and move toward existence with appreciation, liberality, and strength. With devotion, assurance, and an uplifting outlook, you can release your maximum capacity and make the existence of your fantasies.

Systems for Flourishing in a Serious Market

In the present speedy and consistently changing business scene, contest is wild, and standing apart from the group requires vital reasoning, advancement, and flexibility. Whether you're a little startup or an enormous partnership, flourishing in a cutthroat market requires a mix of market examination, client concentration, separation, and deftness. In this thorough aide, we will investigate demonstrated procedures and strategies for flourishing in a serious market, covering key regions, for example, statistical surveying, item separation, client experience, showcasing, and development. By carrying out these systems actually, you can situate your business for progress and beat the opposition in even the hardest economic situations.

Statistical surveying and Investigation

One of the most vital phases in flourishing in a cutthroat market is leading exhaustive statistical surveying and examination to figure out the elements, patterns, and serious scene of your industry. Statistical surveying includes assembling and breaking down information on market size, development potential, client necessities and inclinations, contender procedures, and administrative climate, among different elements.

Market examination empowers you to recognize valuable open doors for development and extension, as well as expected dangers and difficulties that might influence your business. By understanding the requirements and wants of your objective clients, you can foster items and administrations that impact them and separate your image from rivals. Besides, by observing contender exercises and industry patterns, you can remain on the ball and proactively answer changes on the lookout, subsequently keeping an upper hand.

Item Separation

One more key system for flourishing in a serious market is item separation — making remarkable offers that recognize your items or administrations from those of contenders and resound with your objective clients. Item separation can take many structures, including predominant quality, inventive elements, serious evaluating, extraordinary client support, areas of strength for and personality.

To separate your items really, it's fundamental to grasp the requirements, inclinations, and trouble spots of your objective clients and foster items or administrations that address these necessities in an extraordinary and convincing manner. This might include putting resources into innovative work to make inventive arrangements, teaming up with providers and accomplices to upgrade item quality and execution, or utilizing innovation to further develop the client experience and smooth out tasks.

In addition, viable item separation requires progressing observing and transformation to changes in client inclinations, market patterns, and serious elements. By remaining sensitive to the advancing necessities and wants of your objective clients, you can ceaselessly refine and upgrade your items or administrations to keep up with their importance and seriousness on the lookout.

Client Experience

In the present hyper-cutthroat market, giving an uncommon client experience is fundamental for flourishing and separating your image from rivals. Client experience envelops each connection that a client has with your image, from starting contact to post-buy backing, and assumes a huge part in forming discernments, steadfastness, and support.

To convey an outstanding client experience, it's fundamental to focus on client requirements and inclinations and plan items, administrations, and cycles that meet or surpass their assumptions. This might include putting resources into preparing and advancement to guarantee that cutting edge workers have the right stuff and information to convey remarkable assistance, executing innovation answers for smooth out the client venture and further develop productivity, or requesting input and experiences from clients to distinguish regions for development and development.

Besides, building solid associations with clients and encouraging a culture of trust, straightforwardness, and responsiveness can likewise improve the client experience and separate your image from rivals. By paying attention to client input, tending to worries speedily, and doing an amazing job to surpass assumptions, you can assemble dedication, promotion, and long haul connections that drive rehash business and references.

Showcasing and Marking

Compelling showcasing and marking are fundamental for flourishing in a serious market and laying out your image character, notoriety, and presence in the personalities of buyers. Showcasing envelops a great many exercises, including promoting, advertising, web-based entertainment, content showcasing, and experiential showcasing, and assumes an essential part in drawing in, connecting with, and holding clients.

To hang out in a serious market, it's fundamental to foster areas of strength for a personality and incentive that resounds with your objective clients and separates your image from rivals. This might include characterizing your image's main goal, values, and character, making a convincing brand story and visual personality, and imparting your one of a kind incentive reliably across all showcasing channels and touchpoints.

Additionally, utilizing information and investigation to portion your interest group, customize informing, and upgrade advertising efforts can likewise improve the viability and effectiveness of your showcasing endeavors. By fitting your informing and content to the particular necessities and inclinations of various client sections, you can expand pertinence, commitment, and change rates, subsequently amplifying the profit from venture of your showcasing drives.

Advancement and Versatility

Development and flexibility are basic for flourishing in a serious market and remaining on top of things in a steadily changing business scene. Advancement includes growing novel thoughts, items, administrations, or cycles that make an incentive for clients and separate your image from rivals, while flexibility includes answering rapidly and actually to changes on the lookout, client inclinations, and cutthroat elements.

To cultivate development and flexibility inside your association, it's fundamental to make a culture that energizes trial and error, inventiveness, and hazard taking, and rewards workers for rocking the boat and investigating groundbreaking thoughts. This might include putting resources into innovative work, encouraging cross-useful cooperation and information sharing, or making motivations and awards for development and greatness.

Additionally, embracing arising advancements and patterns, for example, man-made consciousness, AI, blockchain, and the web of things, can likewise assist you with remaining on the ball and profit by new open doors for development and separation. By consistently checking market patterns and client inclinations, exploring different avenues regarding new advances and plans of action, and adjusting rapidly to changes in the serious scene, you can situate your business for long haul achievement and manageability.

Flourishing in a serious market requires a blend of vital reasoning, development, client concentration, and flexibility. By directing careful statistical surveying and examination, separating your items or administrations, conveying excellent client encounters, executing viable promoting and marking procedures, and cultivating a culture of development and versatility, you can situate your business for progress and outflank the opposition in even the hardest economic situations.

Thus, as you explore the difficulties and chances of the serious market, make sure to keep fixed on your clients' necessities and inclinations, embrace change and development, and persistently endeavor to separate your image and convey excellent worth. With devotion, imagination, and an eagerness to adjust, you can flourish and prevail in any market climate.

Systems for Maintainable Achievement

Chasing after progress, maintainability is vital. While accomplishing momentary objectives and achievements is significant, supporting accomplishment over the long haul requires an essential methodology that adjusts development, benefit, and social obligation. Whether you're a business visionary, business pioneer, or individual taking a stab at outcome in your own or proficient life, embracing procedures for feasible achievement can assist you with building an establishment for long haul thriving and satisfaction. In this far reaching guide, we will investigate demonstrated procedures and methods for making practical progress, covering key regions like administration, advancement, hierarchical culture, social obligation, and self-awareness. By carrying out these methodologies really, you can make a way to maintainable achievement that benefits you and your association as well as adds to the overall benefit of society.

Authority

At the core of maintainable achievement is compelling administration — visionary, moral, and comprehensive initiative that moves and enables others to accomplish their maximum capacity and add to the aggregate progress of the association. Reasonable achievement starts with initiative that sets an unmistakable vision, values, and bearing for the association, and develops a culture of trust, straightforwardness, and responsibility.

One procedure for cultivating supportable accomplishment through initiative is to show others how its done, exhibiting honesty, lowliness, and a guarantee to greatness in all parts of your work and collaborations. By encapsulating the qualities and ways of behaving that you wish to find in others, you can motivate trust and certainty and make a positive hierarchical culture that encourages cooperation, development, and elite execution.

Besides, viable initiative likewise includes enabling and creating others, cultivating a culture of constant learning and development, and giving open doors to workers to foster their abilities, gifts, and administration potential. By putting resources into administration improvement programs, mentorship drives, and ability the executives methodologies, you can develop a pipeline of future pioneers who are prepared to drive economical achievement and convey the association forward into what's in store.

Advancement

Advancement is one more key driver of maintainable achievement — consistent development that empowers associations to adjust to changing business sector elements, expect client needs, and remain in front of the opposition. Feasible achievement requires a culture of development that empowers imagination, trial and error, and hazard taking, and rewards representatives for rocking the boat and investigating novel thoughts.

One system for encouraging advancement is to establish cross-practical groups and cooperative conditions where workers from various foundations and disciplines can meet up to conceptualize thoughts, take care of issues, and foster inventive arrangements. By separating storehouses and encouraging coordinated effort across divisions and capabilities, you can use the different viewpoints and skill of your colleagues to drive advancement and accomplish advancement results.

Besides, putting resources into innovative work, innovation, and foundation can likewise assist with cultivating development and make a culture of consistent improvement and headway. By keeping up to date with arising advances, patterns, and market potential open doors, and putting resources into the devices and assets expected to exploit them, you can situate your association for long haul achievement and maintainability in a quickly impacting world.

Hierarchical Culture

Hierarchical culture assumes a basic part in reasonable achievement — a culture that qualities and advances variety, value, consideration, and worker prosperity encourages commitment, imagination, and development, and drives execution and results. Practical achievement requires a culture of trust, regard, and cooperation where representatives feel esteemed, upheld, and engaged to carry their full selves to work and add to the outcome of the association.

One methodology for developing a positive hierarchical culture is to focus on variety, value, and incorporation (DEI) drives that advance variety of thought, foundation, and experience, and make a feeling of having a place and acknowledgment for all representatives. By encouraging a culture of inclusivity and having a place, you can take advantage of the maximum capacity of your labor force and release inventiveness, development, and execution across the association.

Besides, putting resources into representative prosperity and balance between serious and fun activities can likewise add to a positive hierarchical culture and supportable achievement. By offering adaptable work game plans, wellbeing projects, and expert improvement open doors, you can uphold the physical, mental, and close to home soundness of your representatives and make a culture that qualities and focuses on their prosperity.

Social Obligation

Social obligation is one more key mainstay of maintainable achievement — associations that are focused on having a beneficial outcome on society and the climate add to everyone's benefit as well as construct trust, dependability, and generosity with clients, workers, and partners. Feasible achievement requires a pledge to corporate social obligation (CSR) drives that address key social and ecological issues and add to the prosperity of networks and the planet.

One methodology for coordinating social obligation into your strategic approaches is to adjust CSR drives to your basic beliefs, mission, and business goals, and focus on drives that are significant, important, and effective for your partners. By zeroing in on regions where your association can have the best effect and utilizing your special assets and assets, you can augment the effect of your CSR endeavors and drive positive change on the planet.

Besides, captivating representatives and partners in CSR drives can likewise improve their feeling of direction, pride, and obligation to the association, and encourage a culture of social obligation and aggregate activity. By including workers in volunteer exercises, local area administration ventures, and manageability drives, you can fortify connections, construct fellowship, and move a common feeling of direction and mission that drives practical achievement.

Self-improvement

At long last, maintainable achievement starts with self-improvement — nonstop learning, development, and personal growth that empowers people to understand their maximum capacity and accomplish their objectives and desires. Maintainable achievement requires a pledge to deep rooted learning and improvement, and a readiness to put resources into oneself and develop the abilities, information, and mentality expected to flourish in a quickly impacting world.

One procedure for self-awareness is to set clear, feasible objectives and foster an arrangement for accomplishing them, including distinguishing regions for development, searching out learning open doors, and focusing on continuous development and improvement. By taking responsibility for individual and expert turn of events and putting resources into yourself, you can upgrade your abilities, extend your chances, and open additional opportunities for progress and satisfaction.

Additionally, searching out tutors, mentors, and good examples can likewise speed up your self-awareness and give significant direction, backing, and input as you explore your excursion to progress. By gaining from the encounters and experiences of other people who have made progress in their own lives and vocations, you can acquire significant viewpoint, shrewdness, and motivation that can assist you with defeating difficulties, immediately take advantage of chances, and accomplish your objectives.

Manageable achievement requires an essential methodology that adjusts development, benefit, and social obligation, and focuses on initiative, advancement, hierarchical culture, social obligation, and self-awareness. By embracing methodologies for maintainable achievement and developing a culture of greatness, honesty, and advancement, you can fabricate an establishment for long haul flourishing and satisfaction that benefits you, your association, and society overall.

In this way, as you take a stab at progress in your own and proficient life, make sure to focus on authority, development, hierarchical culture, social obligation, and self-awareness, and focus on persistent learning, development, and improvement. By embracing these standards and systems, you can make a way to reasonable achievement that benefits you and your association as well as adds to the long term benefit of society and the planet.

Chapter 4:

Strategies for Sustainable Expansion

Growing a business can be both invigorating and testing. While development presents open doors for expanded income and portion of the overall industry, it additionally brings dangers and intricacies that can compromise the supportability of the business on the off chance that not oversaw actually. Maintainable extension requires cautious preparation, vital reasoning, and an emphasis on long haul reasonability and effect. In this aide, we will investigate demonstrated methodologies and strategies for accomplishing practical development in the business field, covering key regions like market examination, versatility, advancement, risk the board, and partner commitment. By executing these methodologies actually, organizations can explore development with reason and benefit, guaranteeing long haul achievement and supportability.

Market Investigation

Prior to leaving on any extension drive, it's crucial for direct an intensive market examination to grasp the valuable open doors, difficulties, and dangers related with venture into new business sectors or fragments. Market examination includes assembling and dissecting information on market size, development potential, client requirements and inclinations, serious elements, administrative climate, and other pertinent variables.

One system for leading business sector examination is to use both quantitative and subjective exploration techniques to assemble experiences into market patterns, client conduct, and contender procedures. Quantitative strategies, like studies, information investigation, and market displaying, can give important information on market size, socioeconomics, and purchasing conduct, while subjective techniques, for example, interviews, center gatherings, and ethnographic examination, can give further experiences into client requirements, inspirations, and trouble spots.

In addition, it's fundamental to evaluate the cutthroat scene and distinguish possible hindrances to passage or rivalry that might affect the progress of development endeavors. By figuring out the qualities, shortcomings, open doors, and dangers presented by contenders, organizations can foster systems to separate themselves and cut out a remarkable situation on the lookout.

Adaptability

Versatility is one more basic component to consider while making arrangements for economical development. Versatility alludes to the capacity of a business to develop and adjust to expanded request or changing economic situations without compromising quality, effectiveness, or benefit. Practical development requires versatile plans of action, cycles, and framework that can uphold development while keeping up with functional greatness and consumer loyalty.

One methodology for accomplishing adaptability is to plan business cycles and frameworks that are adaptable, versatile, and ready to oblige changes in volume, intricacy, and extension. This might include putting resources into innovation and computerization to smooth out activities, further develop productivity, and lessen costs, or executing adaptable plans of action, for example, membership based evaluating or stage based plans of action, that can uphold quick development and extension.

Besides, it's fundamental for fabricate areas of strength for a culture and ability pipeline that can uphold development and adjust to changing requirements and needs. By putting resources into worker preparing and advancement, authority improvement projects, and execution the executives frameworks, organizations can guarantee that their groups have what it takes, information, and abilities expected to drive feasible development and convey worth to clients and partners.

Development

Development is one more key driver of feasible extension — consistent advancement that empowers organizations to separate themselves, enter new business sectors, and make an incentive for clients and partners. Reasonable development requires a culture of development that empowers imagination, trial and error, and hazard taking, and rewards representatives for rocking the boat and investigating groundbreaking thoughts.

One methodology for cultivating advancement is to establish cross-utilitarian groups and cooperative conditions where workers from various foundations and disciplines can meet up to conceptualize thoughts, take care of issues, and foster imaginative arrangements. By encouraging a culture of coordinated effort and information sharing, organizations can use the different points of view and skill of their groups to drive development and accomplish advancement results.

Besides, putting resources into innovative work, innovation, and foundation can likewise assist with encouraging development and make a culture of constant improvement and headway. By keeping up to date with arising innovations, patterns, and market potential open doors, and putting resources into the devices and assets expected to benefit from them, organizations can situate themselves for long haul achievement and maintainability in a quickly impacting world.

Risk The board

Extension intrinsically implies chances, and dealing with these dangers actually is fundamental for economical development and achievement. Maintainable extension requires a proactive way to deal with risk the executives that expects possible dangers, surveys their effect and probability, and creates methodologies to successfully relieve or oversee them.

One procedure for overseeing gambles related with development is to direct an extensive gamble evaluation to distinguish expected dangers and weaknesses and focus on them in light of their seriousness and probability. This might imply surveying gambles with connected with market unpredictability, administrative consistence, store network interruptions, online protection dangers, or international unsteadiness, among others.

In addition, it's fundamental to foster alternate courses of action and hazard relief techniques to address likely dangers and limit their effect on business tasks and execution. By creating elective situations, reaction plans, and emergency the board conventions, organizations can guarantee that they are ready to answer actually to surprising occasions and limit disturbances to their activities and partners.

Partner Commitment

At last, practical extension requires viable partner commitment — building connections and associations with key partners, including clients, representatives, providers, financial backers, controllers, and networks, to make shared esteem and common advantage. Feasible extension includes adjusting the requirements and interests of all partners and guaranteeing that development endeavors are lined up with their assumptions and needs.

One technique for partner commitment is to embrace a cooperative methodology that includes partners in the dynamic cycle and looks for info and criticism from them on extension plans and drives. By including partners early and frequently, organizations can fabricate trust, straightforwardness, and purchase in for extension endeavors and guarantee that they address the requirements and worries of all gatherings included.

In addition, it's fundamental to impart straightforwardly and straightforwardly with partners about development plans, dangers, and open doors, and to request their feedback and criticism in the meantime. By keeping up with open lines of correspondence and drawing in partners in discourse and navigation, organizations can construct more grounded connections, improve trust and validity, and make a strong biological system that cultivates supportable development and achievement.

In economical development it's requires cautious preparation, vital reasoning, and an emphasis on long haul feasibility and effect. By leading careful market examination, focusing on versatility and development, overseeing gambles really, and drawing in partners cooperatively, organizations can explore development with reason and productivity, guaranteeing long haul achievement and supportability.

In this way, as you set out on your excursion of extension in the business field, make sure to focus on manageability, partner commitment, and development, and to move toward development with an essential mentality and a pledge to making an incentive for all partners included. With devotion, imagination, and an emphasis on long haul influence, you can accomplish practical development and construct an establishment for enduring achievement and success.

Scaling Your Business

Scaling a business includes something other than expanding income — it requires an essential way to deal with development and extension that guarantees supportability, productivity, and long haul achievement. Whether you're a startup hoping to speed up development or a laid out business looking to venture into new business sectors or areas, scaling requires cautious preparation, asset distribution, and execution. In this thorough aide, we will investigate demonstrated procedures and strategies for scaling your business, covering key regions like market examination, functional productivity, client obtaining, ability the board, and monetary administration. By carrying out these procedures really, you can situate your business for supportable development and extension, guaranteeing progress in the present serious commercial center.

Market Examination

Prior to setting out on any scaling drive, it's fundamental for direct an intensive market investigation to grasp the potential open doors, difficulties, and dangers related with development and extension. Market examination includes assembling and breaking down information on market size, development potential, client necessities and inclinations, serious elements, administrative climate, and other important variables.

One system for directing business sector investigation is to use both quantitative and subjective examination techniques to assemble bits of knowledge into market patterns, client conduct, and contender procedures. Quantitative techniques, like reviews, information examination, and market demonstrating, can give significant information on market size, socioeconomics, and purchasing conduct, while subjective strategies, for example, interviews, center gatherings, and ethnographic exploration, can give further experiences into client necessities, inspirations, and trouble spots.

Also, it's fundamental to evaluate the serious scene and recognize possible hindrances to passage or rivalry that might affect the progress of scaling endeavors. By grasping the qualities, shortcomings, open doors, and dangers presented by contenders, organizations can foster systems to separate themselves and cut out a novel situation on the lookout.

Functional Effectiveness

Functional effectiveness is basic for scaling your business — smoothing out processes, lessening costs, and further developing efficiency to help development and extension. Reasonable scaling requires versatile plans of action, cycles, and framework that can uphold expanded volume, intricacy, and extension while keeping up with quality, productivity, and consumer loyalty.

One technique for accomplishing functional effectiveness is to recognize and kill shortcomings and bottlenecks in your activities through process enhancement, robotization, and innovation reception. By utilizing innovation arrangements, for example, undertaking asset arranging (ERP) frameworks, client relationship the executives (CRM) programming, and work process mechanization instruments, organizations can smooth out tasks, further develop correspondence and cooperation, and lessen manual exertion and mistakes.

In addition, it's fundamental to put resources into preparing and advancement to guarantee that representatives have what it takes, information, and capacities expected to help development and extension. By giving continuous preparation and upskilling open doors, organizations can engage representatives to perform at their best and add to the progress of scaling drives.

Client Procurement

Client procurement is one more key driver of scaling your business — obtaining new clients and extending your client base to drive income development and piece of the pie. Economical scaling requires an essential way to deal with client obtaining that spotlights on recognizing and focusing on high-esteem clients, enhancing promoting and deals processes, and conveying outstanding client encounters.

One procedure for client procurement is to use information and investigation to recognize and focus on high-esteem client fragments and foster designated promoting and deals methodologies to contact them. By dissecting client information, like socioeconomics, ways of behaving, and inclinations, organizations can tailor their promoting messages and offers to reverberate with the necessities and wants of their ideal interest group and increment transformation rates.

In addition, it's fundamental to put resources into client relationship the board (CRM) frameworks and deals enablement devices to follow client collaborations, oversee leads and open doors, and furnish outreach groups with the experiences and assets they need to close arrangements actually. By enabling outreach groups with the right devices and data, organizations can smooth out the deals interaction, further develop effectiveness, and drive income development.

Ability The board

Ability the board is basic for scaling your business — building a high-performing group that can uphold development and extension and drive advancement and greatness. Feasible scaling requires an essential way to deal with ability the board that spotlights on drawing in, creating, and holding top ability and cultivating a culture of cooperation, imagination, and consistent improvement.

One system for ability the board is to characterize clear jobs and obligations and foster an ability procurement methodology that lines up with your business goals and development plans. By distinguishing the abilities, information, and experience expected to help scaling drives, organizations can draw in and recruit the right ability to fill key jobs and drive achievement.

In addition, it's fundamental to put resources into representative turn of events and commitment to guarantee that workers have the right stuff, inspiration, and potential open doors they need to flourish and develop inside the association. By giving continuous preparation, tutoring, and profession advancement valuable open doors, organizations can enable representatives to arrive at their maximum capacity and add to the outcome of scaling drives.

Monetary Administration

Monetary administration is urgent for scaling your business — guaranteeing that you have the assets and capital expected to help development and extension and oversee gambles really. Practical scaling requires an essential way to deal with monetary administration that spotlights on enhancing income, overseeing costs, and getting to funding to fuel development.

One technique for monetary administration is to foster a definite monetary arrangement and financial plan that frames your income projections, costs, and capital necessities for scaling drives. By estimating your monetary requirements and distinguishing possible wellsprings of financing, organizations can guarantee that they have the assets and capital expected to help development and extension and oversee gambles really.

Also, it's crucial for screen and oversee income near guarantee that you have the liquidity expected to help everyday activities and interest in scaling drives. By executing income the executives systems, like invoicing instantly, overseeing receivables and payables actually, and keeping up with satisfactory stores, organizations can limit the gamble of income deficiencies and guarantee monetary strength and maintainability.

Furthermore, scaling your business requires an essential methodology that includes market investigation, functional productivity, client securing, ability the executives, and monetary administration. By carrying out these systems really, organizations can explore development and extension with reason and benefit, guaranteeing long haul achievement and maintainability in the present cutthroat commercial center.

In this way, as you leave on your excursion of scaling your business, make sure to focus on essential preparation, asset portion, and execution, and to move toward development with an emphasis on long haul practicality and effect. With devotion, imagination, and a guarantee to greatness, you can accomplish supportable scaling and position your business for outcome in the years to come.

Instruments for Proficiency and Development

In the present quick moving and cutthroat business climate, effectiveness and development are vital for progress. Organizations should persistently endeavor to smooth out tasks, increment efficiency, and drive development to remain on the ball and accomplish reasonable development. Luckily, progressions in innovation have given organizations a wide cluster of devices and answers for assist them with accomplishing these objectives. From project the executives programming to client relationship the board (CRM) frameworks to man-made consciousness (computer based intelligence) and AI, there are incalculable apparatuses accessible to organizations to further develop effectiveness and drive development. In this exhaustive aide, we will investigate probably the best apparatuses for proficiency and development in the business community, covering key regions like efficiency, joint effort, client commitment, examination, and robotization. By utilizing these apparatuses actually, organizations can open new degrees of effectiveness, efficiency, and development, situating themselves for long haul outcome in the present computerized economy.

Efficiency Instruments

1. Project The board Programming: Venture the executives programming like Asana, Trello, or Monday.com assists organizations with coordinating assignments, track progress, and team up successfully on projects. These devices permit groups to set cutoff times, appoint assignments, share records, and impart continuously, smoothing out project work processes and further developing efficiency.

2. Time Following Programming: Time following programming like Toggl or Reap empowers organizations to screen representative time spent on undertakings and tasks precisely. By following time spent on different exercises, organizations can distinguish failures, apportion assets all the more successfully, and further develop time usage across the association.

3. Task Robotization Devices: Undertaking mechanization apparatuses, for example, Zapier or IFTTT permit organizations to computerize redundant errands and work processes, diminishing manual exertion and further developing proficiency. These apparatuses empower organizations to make computerized work processes that interface different applications and administrations, setting off activities in view of predefined conditions or occasions.

4. Specialized Apparatuses: Specialized instruments like Leeway or Microsoft Groups work with continuous correspondence and joint effort among colleagues, no matter what their area. These apparatuses offer elements, for example, texting, video conferencing, record sharing, and venture channels, empowering groups to convey really and remain associated all through the normal working day.

Cooperation Apparatuses

1. Archive Joint effort Programming: Record cooperation programming like Google Work area (previously G Suite) or Microsoft Office 365 permits groups to make, alter, and team up on reports, bookkeeping sheets, and introductions progressively. These apparatuses empower different clients to chip away at a similar record at the same time, further developing cooperation and efficiency.

2. Distributed storage Arrangements: Distributed storage arrangements like Dropbox, Google Drive, or Microsoft OneDrive give organizations secure and adaptable capacity for records and reports. These instruments permit groups to get to records from anyplace, on any gadget, and team up on archives consistently, improving adaptability and joint effort.

3. Virtual Joint effort Stages: Virtual cooperation stages like Zoom, Microsoft Groups, or Cisco Webex empower remote groups to team up successfully through video conferencing, screen sharing, and virtual gathering rooms. These devices work with virtual coordinated effort and correspondence, empowering groups to cooperate consistently no matter what their area.

4. Work process The executives Programming: Work process the board programming, for example, Airtable or Kissflow helps organizations mechanize and smooth out processes, from project the board to HR to deals and advertising. These apparatuses empower organizations to plan custom work processes, mechanize dreary undertakings, and track progress continuously, further developing proficiency and efficiency.

Client Commitment Devices

Client Relationship 1. The executives (CRM) Programming: CRM programming like Salesforce, HubSpot, or Zoho CRM empowers organizations to oversee client connections, track associations, and examine client information successfully. These apparatuses assist organizations with smoothing out deals and advertising processes, customize interchanges, and further develop consumer loyalty and maintenance.

2. Email Showcasing Stages: Email advertising stages like Mailchimp, Consistent Contact, or Sendinblue empower organizations to make, send, and track email crusades productively. These apparatuses offer elements, for example, email layouts, computerization, division, and examination, assisting organizations with drawing in clients, support leads, and drive transformations.

3. Web-based Entertainment The executives Apparatuses: Online entertainment the board devices like Hootsuite, Cradle, or Fledgling Social assist organizations with dealing with their virtual entertainment presence across different stages. These instruments empower organizations to plan posts, screen notices and discussions, break down commitment measurements, and measure the adequacy of their web-based entertainment endeavors.

4. Client service Programming: Client service programming like Zendesk, Freshdesk, or Radio empowers organizations to offer opportune and customized help to clients through different channels, including email, talk, telephone, and online entertainment. These devices assist organizations with settling client requests proficiently, track support tickets, and measure consumer loyalty.

Examination Apparatuses

1. Business Knowledge (BI) Stages: Business insight stages like Scene, Power BI, or Google Information Studio empower organizations to successfully dissect and picture information. These instruments assist organizations with pursuing information driven choices by changing crude information into noteworthy experiences and dashboards, empowering partners to screen execution, distinguish patterns, and track KPIs.

2 Web Investigation Arrangements: Web examination arrangements like Google Investigation or Adobe Investigation give organizations significant experiences into site traffic, client conduct, and transformation rates. These apparatuses assist organizations with understanding how clients connect with their site, advance promoting efforts, and further develop the client experience to drive commitment and transformations.

3. Showcasing Mechanization Stages: Promoting robotization stages like Marketo, Pardot, or ActiveCampaign empower organizations to computerize advertising processes, including email promoting, lead supporting, and mission the executives. These apparatuses assist organizations with smoothing out showcasing work processes, customize correspondences, and track crusade execution, driving effectiveness and return for capital invested.

4. Prescient Examination Programming: Prescient investigation programming like IBM Watson Examination or RapidMiner empowers organizations to estimate future patterns and results in view of authentic information and factual calculations. These devices assist organizations with expecting client conduct, distinguish valuable open doors, and relieve chances, empowering more educated navigation and vital preparation.

Computerization Devices

1. Mechanical Interaction Robotization (RPA) Programming: Mechanical cycle mechanization programming like UiPath, Computerization Anyplace, or Blue Crystal empowers organizations to robotize dull and run based assignments across frameworks and applications. These apparatuses assist organizations with further developing effectiveness, lessen mistakes, and let loose workers to zero in on more key and worth added exercises.

2. Chatbots and Remote helpers: Chatbots and menial helpers controlled by computer based intelligence and regular language handling (NLP) innovation empower organizations to mechanize client associations and backing requests. These instruments can deal with routine client requests, give customized proposals, and help with errands like booking arrangements or handling orders, further developing productivity and consumer loyalty.

3. Work process Computerization Stages: Work process mechanization stages like Kissflow, Zapier, or Workato empower organizations to robotize complex work processes and incorporate different frameworks and applications. These instruments assist organizations with smoothing out processes, lessen manual exertion, and further develop consistency and precision across the association, driving proficiency and efficiency.

4. Artificial intelligence Controlled Devices: computer based intelligence fueled instruments, for example, AI calculations, prescient investigation, and normal language handling (NLP) empower organizations to robotize and streamline different assignments and cycles, from deals and promoting to client assistance and activities. These devices assist organizations with examining information, make forecasts, and customize communications, empowering more compelling independent direction and further developing the client experience.

In utilizing innovation devices for proficiency and development is fundamental for organizations to remain cutthroat and drive progress in the present advanced economy. From efficiency apparatuses to coordinated effort stages to client commitment answers for investigation and robotization instruments, there are endless choices accessible to organizations to smooth out tasks, further develop efficiency, and drive advancement. By distinguishing the right devices for their necessities and executing them really, organizations can open new degrees of proficiency, efficiency, and development, situating themselves for long haul achievement and supportability.

Thus, as the need might arise and objectives, consider utilizing innovation instruments to drive effectiveness and development across your association. Whether you're hoping to smooth out tasks, further develop coordinated effort, connect with clients all the more really, or gain significant bits of knowledge from information, there's many apparatuses accessible to assist you with accomplishing your targets and drive progress in the present unique business climate.

Consulting Gold

Chapter 5:

Strategies for Maximizing Your Earnings

In the present dynamic and cutthroat business climate, boosting your profit is fundamental for making monetary progress and creating financial stability. Whether you're a business person, specialist, or worker, there are different methodologies you can utilize to build your pay and augment your procuring potential. From arranging more significant compensations to differentiating revenue streams to effective money management astutely, there are endless ways of helping your income and accomplish your monetary objectives. In this complete aide, we will investigate the absolute best procedures for expanding your profit, covering key regions like professional success, business venture, recurring, automated revenue, speculation, and monetary preparation. By carrying out these methodologies successfully, you can open new open doors for monetary development and thriving, making ready for a more splendid monetary future.

Professional success

1. Arranging More significant compensations: One of the most immediate methods for expanding your profit is to arrange more significant compensations and remuneration bundles. Prior to entering exchanges, research industry guidelines and benchmarks for your job and level of involvement, and feature your achievements, abilities, and incentive to legitimize your ideal compensation. By pushing for yourself really and showing your value to businesses, you can get higher pay and increment your income fundamentally.

2. Putting resources into Schooling and Ability Improvement: Putting resources into training and expertise advancement can likewise upgrade your acquiring expected by expanding your worth in the commercial center. Think about seeking after postgraduate educations, confirmations, or expert improvement courses that line up with your profession objectives and yearnings. By consistently overhauling your abilities and information, you can situate yourself for more lucrative jobs and progression potential open doors in your field.

3. Looking for Advancements and Headway Open doors: Proactively looking for advancements and progression valuable open doors inside your association can likewise assist with expanding your profit. Express your advantage in vocation development to your bosses, take on extra obligations and difficulties, and search out amazing open doors for proficient turn of events and mentorship. By exhibiting your initiative potential and obligation to progress, you can situate yourself for advancement and higher procuring expected inside your ongoing association.

Business

1. Beginning a Business: Business venture offers boundless procuring potential for those able to face challenges and seek after their interests. Consider going into business or sending off a part time job in a specialty market or industry where you have skill and premium. Whether it's an independent counseling business, an internet business store, or a tech startup, business venture permits you to control your procuring potential and create financial stability based on your conditions.

2. Making Various Revenue Sources: Differentiating your revenue streams is one more compelling methodology for expanding your income as a business visionary. Investigate potential chances to adapt your abilities, mastery, and resources through different channels, for example, counseling, partner promoting, online courses, or investment properties. By making various surges of pay, you can lessen dependence on any single wellspring of income and increment your generally speaking acquiring potential.

3. Scaling Your Business: Scaling your business is fundamental for opening outstanding development and expanding your profit as a business visionary. Put resources into procedures and assets to extend your scope, increment your client base, and develop your income, like showcasing and promoting, mechanization and rethinking, and vital organizations. By scaling your business actually, you can open new degrees of productivity and monetary achievement.

Recurring, automated revenue

1. Putting resources into Land: Land effective money management offers valuable open doors for producing automated revenue through investment properties, land speculation trusts (REITs), or crowdfunding stages. Consider putting resources into pay creating properties or REITs that produce consistent income through rental pay or profits. By building an arrangement of pay producing resources, you can make recurring sources of income that supplement your profit and create long haul financial momentum.

2. Profit Stocks and Bonds: Profit stocks and bonds are one more choice for producing recurring, automated revenue and expanding your income. Put resources into blue-chip stocks or profit paying common subsidizes that disperse standard profits to investors. Moreover, consider designating a part of your venture portfolio to bonds or fixed-pay protections that proposition consistent interest installments. By reinvesting profits and premium income, you can speed up the development of your venture portfolio and increment your recurring, automated revenue over the long haul.

3. Computerized Resources and Protected innovation: Advanced resources and protected innovation offer open doors for creating recurring, automated revenue through sovereignties, authorizing expenses, or computerized item deals. Consider making and adapting computerized resources, for example, digital books, online courses, stock photography, or programming applications. By utilizing your aptitude and imagination to make important advanced items, you can produce recurring sources of income that keep on bringing in cash long after the underlying speculation of time and assets.

Speculation

1. Securities exchange Financial planning: Financial exchange money management offers amazing open doors for expanding your profit through capital appreciation and profits. Consider putting resources into a broadened arrangement of stocks or value common supports that line up with your venture objectives and chance resilience. Center around long haul development and worth money management standards, and consistently survey and rebalance your portfolio to advance returns and limit risk.

2. Retirement Records: Retirement records, for example, 401(k)s, IRAs, or Roth IRAs give charge advantaged chances to expanding your profit and creating long haul financial stability. Exploit boss supported retirement designs and contribute the most extreme admissible sum every year to expand charge conceded development and self multiplying dividends. Also, think about opening and adding to a singular retirement account (IRA) or Roth IRA to enhance your retirement reserve funds and broaden your venture portfolio.

3. Elective Speculations: Elective speculations, for example, confidential value, mutual funds, or investment offer open doors for expanding your income through better yields and enhancement. Consider dispensing a piece of your venture portfolio to elective speculations that offer openness to forward thinking resource classes and venture systems. Nonetheless, be aware of the dangers related with elective speculations and talk with a monetary counsel to guarantee they line up with your venture goals and chance resistance.

Monetary Preparation

1. Planning and Cost Administration: Powerful planning and cost administration are fundamental for boosting your income and accomplishing monetary objectives. Track your pay and costs cautiously, make a spending plan that lines up with your monetary needs and goals, and recognize regions where you can diminish optional spending and set aside cash. By living inside your means and focusing on reserve funds and ventures, you can boost your profit and create financial stability over the long run.

2. Obligation The board and FICO assessment Improvement: Overseeing obligation really and further developing your financial assessment can likewise assist with augmenting your income and monetary open doors. Foster an arrangement to settle exorbitant premium obligation methodicallly, focus on obligations with the most noteworthy loan costs first, and investigate choices for solidifying or renegotiating obligation to bring down financing costs. Also, screen your FICO rating routinely, and do whatever it takes to further develop it by covering bills on time, diminishing Visa adjusts, and staying away from new obligation.

3. Monetary Counsel and Expense Arranging: Working with a monetary consultant and duty organizer can give important direction and backing to boosting your profit and enhancing what is happening. Search out proficient counsel on speculation systems, retirement arranging, charge advancement, and home intending to guarantee that you're going with informed choices and augmenting your monetary open doors. By utilizing the mastery and bits of knowledge of monetary experts, you can explore complex monetary choices and accomplish your monetary objectives with certainty.

In boosting your profit it requires a blend of key preparation, proactive direction, and trained execution. Whether you're centered around propelling your vocation, beginning a business, producing recurring, automated revenue, contributing shrewdly, or dealing with your funds successfully, there are incalculable chances to expand your pay and accomplish your monetary objectives. By carrying out the techniques framed in this guide really and reliably, you can open new degrees of monetary achievement and success, preparing for a more splendid monetary future.

Along these lines, as you set out on your excursion to expand your profit, make sure to remain fixed on your objectives, remain trained in your methodology, and remain proactive in searching out new open doors for development and headway. With devotion, constancy, and a guarantee to monetary achievement, you can accomplish your objectives and construct the existence of your fantasies.

Procedures for Conquering Difficulties

In the dynamic and cutthroat universe of business, challenges are unavoidable. From financial slumps to mechanical disturbances to showcase contest, organizations face a heap of obstructions that can ruin their development and achievement. Nonetheless, it's the means by which organizations answer these difficulties that eventually decides their strength and life span. By embracing successful systems and approaches, organizations can conquer impediments, adjust to evolving conditions, and arise more grounded than any time in recent memory. In this complete aide, we will investigate the absolute most normal difficulties looked by organizations and procedures for conquering them, covering key regions like authority, development, versatility, and transformation. By executing these procedures successfully, organizations can explore difficulties with certainty and accomplish their objectives in the present powerful business climate.

Authority

1. Viable Correspondence: Successful correspondence is fundamental for defeating difficulties in business. Pioneers should convey obviously, straightforwardly, and reliably with workers, clients, providers, and different partners to guarantee arrangement, assemble trust, and encourage cooperation. By keeping partners educated and connected with, pioneers can limit vulnerability and disarray, and rally support for conquering difficulties on the whole.

2. Vital Preparation: Key arranging is basic for expecting and tending to difficulties before they grow into emergencies. Pioneers ought to foster well thought out plans that framework clear targets, needs, and activity ventures for exploring difficulties successfully. By proactively distinguishing expected deterrents and creating emergency courses of action, pioneers can alleviate dangers and position their organizations for outcome notwithstanding vulnerability.

3. Versatile Authority: Versatile initiative is fundamental for driving through change and vulnerability. Pioneers should be light-footed, adaptable, and receptive to evolving conditions, and able to change procedures and needs depending on the situation. By cultivating a culture of versatility and strength inside their associations, chiefs can engage representatives to embrace change, improve, and conquer difficulties cooperatively.

Development

1. Embracing Imagination: Inventiveness is fundamental for defeating difficulties and driving development in business. Pioneers ought to urge representatives to think inventively, explore different avenues regarding groundbreaking thoughts, and challenge regular reasoning. By encouraging a culture of inventiveness and development, organizations can recognize novel answers for complex issues and remain in front of the opposition.

2. Putting resources into Innovative work: Putting resources into innovative work (Research and development) is pivotal for driving advancement and defeating difficulties in business. Pioneers ought to distribute assets to Research and development drives that investigate new advances, items, and administrations, and address developing business sector patterns and client needs. By keeping up to date with industry improvements and putting resources into advancement, organizations can situate themselves for long haul achievement and flexibility.

3. Cooperative Critical thinking: Cooperative critical thinking includes uniting different viewpoints and aptitude to successfully address difficulties. Pioneers ought to work with cross-utilitarian joint effort and collaboration, energize open exchange and conceptualizing, and engage representatives to contribute thoughts and arrangements. By utilizing the aggregate knowledge of their groups, organizations can distinguish creative ways to deal with conquering difficulties and drive maintainable development.

Flexibility

1. Building Areas of strength for a Culture: major areas of strength for a culture is fundamental for cultivating versatility and conquering difficulties in business. Pioneers ought to develop a culture of trust, straightforwardness, and versatility, where representatives feel upheld, engaged, and propelled to conquer obstructions. By putting resources into worker prosperity and confidence, organizations can assemble versatility and climate misfortune all the more really.

2. Creating The ability to appreciate individuals on a deeper level: The capacity to understand people on a deeper level is basic for exploring difficulties and driving with versatility. Pioneers ought to foster mindfulness, sympathy, and compelling relational abilities to deal with their feelings and those of others during seasons of vulnerability and stress. By encouraging ability to appreciate people on a profound level inside their associations, chiefs can rouse certainty, fabricate trust, and cultivate versatility among representatives.

3. Gaining from Disappointment: Disappointment is an inescapable piece of business, however it can likewise be a significant learning an open door. Pioneers ought to energize a development outlook that sees disappointment as a venturing stone to progress, instead of a mishap. By embracing disappointment, examining underlying drivers, and separating illustrations learned, organizations can adjust their methodologies and cycles to keep away from comparable traps from here on out and fabricate flexibility over the long run.

Variation

1. Spryness and Adaptability: Readiness and adaptability are fundamental for adjusting to changing circumstances and defeating difficulties in business. Pioneers ought to turn rapidly in light of new data or market elements, and engage representatives to do likewise. By cultivating a culture of spryness and adaptability, organizations can profit by open doors and relieve gambles all the more really.

2. Consistent Learning and Improvement: Constant learning and advancement are basic for remaining on top of things and beating difficulties in business. Pioneers ought to put resources into worker preparing and improvement drives that upgrade abilities, information, and capacities across the association. By encouraging a culture of deep rooted learning, organizations can adjust to evolving innovations, market patterns, and client inclinations all the more really.

3. Vital Organizations and Collusions: Key associations and unions can give organizations admittance to assets, mastery, and market open doors that empower them to really conquer difficulties more. Pioneers ought to search out essential associations with correlative organizations, providers, or industry affiliations that offer common advantages and backing shared targets. By utilizing the qualities and assets of their accomplices, organizations can improve their seriousness and strength notwithstanding challenges.

In beating difficulties in business it requires successful administration, development, versatility, and variation. By taking on procedures and approaches that focus on correspondence, imagination, joint effort, and consistent learning, organizations can explore impediments with certainty and accomplish their objectives in the present powerful business climate.

Thus, as you face difficulties in your business process, make sure to embrace imagination, encourage strength, and adjust to changing circumstances with dexterity and adaptability. By driving with vision and reason, putting resources into development and ability improvement, and developing a culture of cooperation and consistent improvement, you can beat impediments and make supportable progress despite misfortune.

Developing Accomplishment from The inside

Progress in business not entirely set in stone by outer factors, for example, economic situations, contest, or financial patterns. All things considered, it is frequently developed from the inside - through the development of a solid groundwork based on guiding principle, culture, initiative, and hierarchical capacities. In this exhaustive aide, we will investigate methodologies for developing accomplishment from the inside, covering key regions like hierarchical culture, authority advancement, worker commitment, and persistent improvement. By zeroing in on these inner variables, organizations can fabricate a strong starting point for development, flexibility, and long haul progress in the present powerful business climate.

Authoritative Culture

1. Characterizing Basic beliefs: Basic beliefs act as the groundwork of authoritative culture, directing navigation, conduct, and collaborations inside the organization. Pioneers ought to characterize basic beliefs that mirror the organization's main goal, vision, and reason, and impart them plainly to workers. By adjusting activities and ways of behaving to guiding principle, organizations can cultivate a positive and firm hierarchical culture that drives achievement.

2. Encouraging Straightforwardness and Trust: Straightforwardness and trust are fundamental components of a solid hierarchical culture. It would be ideal for pioneers to convey transparently and genuinely with workers, sharing data about organization execution, objectives, and difficulties. By cultivating straightforwardness and trust, organizations can areas of strength for construct with representatives, improve spirit, and advance cooperation and development.

3. Empowering Variety and Consideration: Variety and incorporation are basic for encouraging inventiveness, advancement, and strength inside associations. Pioneers ought to make a culture that qualities and celebrates variety in the entirety of its structures, including race, orientation, nationality, age, and foundation. By embracing variety and consideration, organizations can take advantage of a more extensive scope of points of view and thoughts, driving development and upper hand.

4. Advancing Balance between serious and fun activities: Balance between fun and serious activities is fundamental for representative prosperity and efficiency. Pioneers ought to urge representatives to focus on taking care of oneself, put down stopping points among work and individual life, and keep a good overall arrangement among expert and individual obligations. By advancing balance between fun and serious activities, organizations can diminish burnout, increment commitment, and hold top ability.

Authority Advancement

1. Putting resources into Authority Advancement: Administration improvement is basic for developing accomplishment from inside associations. Pioneers ought to put resources into preparing and advancement programs that assist representatives at all levels with creating authority abilities, for example, correspondence, the capacity to understand anyone on a deeper level, independent direction, and compromise. By fostering a pipeline of gifted pioneers, organizations can drive execution, development, and development.

2. Showing others how its done: Chiefs should show others how its done and exhibit the qualities and ways of behaving they anticipate from workers. By demonstrating honesty, responsibility, versatility, and compassion, pioneers can move trust, fabricate validity, and cultivate a positive hierarchical culture. Showing others how its done establishes the vibe for the whole association and supports the significance of fundamental beliefs and moral way of behaving.

3.   Enabling Representatives: Engaging workers to take responsibility for work and pursue choices independently is fundamental for building a culture of responsibility and development. Pioneers ought to assign authority, give independence, and backing representatives in proceeding with carefully weighed out courses of action and investigating groundbreaking thoughts. By enabling representatives, organizations can take advantage of their maximum capacity, drive imagination, and adjust all the more rapidly to change.

4. Giving Mentorship and Instructing: Mentorship and training are significant apparatuses for administration improvement and representative development. Pioneers ought to tutor and mentor workers, giving direction, criticism, and backing to assist them with fostering their abilities and accomplish their objectives. By putting resources into mentorship and training connections, organizations can develop a culture of constant learning and improvement, driving individual and hierarchical achievement.

Representative Commitment

1. Establishing a Positive Workplace: A positive workplace is fundamental for cultivating representative commitment and fulfillment. Pioneers ought to make a culture that qualities and focuses on representative prosperity, acknowledgment, and balance between serious and fun activities. By encouraging a positive workplace, organizations can make everyone feel quite a bit better, increment efficiency, and hold top ability.

2. Advancing Correspondence and Coordinated effort: Correspondence and cooperation are fundamental for driving worker commitment and arrangement. Pioneers ought to energize open correspondence, criticism, and thought dividing between representatives, groups, and divisions. By advancing a culture of cooperation, organizations can separate storehouses, further develop independent direction, and drive advancement.

3. Perceiving and Remunerating Accomplishments: Perceiving and compensating worker accomplishments is fundamental for inspiring and holding top ability. Pioneers ought to recognize and celebrate worker commitments, achievements, and victories consistently. By giving significant acknowledgment and prizes, organizations can lift the general mood, support wanted ways of behaving, and make a culture of appreciation and appreciation.

4. Putting resources into Proficient Turn of events: Proficient improvement amazing open doors are basic for drawing in and holding representatives. Pioneers ought to put resources into preparing, schooling, and vocation improvement programs that assist workers with growing new abilities, develop expertly, and advance their professions inside the association. By putting resources into proficient turn of events, organizations can show a pledge to worker development and achievement, driving commitment and dedication.

Nonstop Improvement

1. Embracing a Development Mentality: A development outlook is fundamental for driving ceaseless improvement and advancement inside associations. Pioneers ought to urge representatives to embrace difficulties, gain from disappointments, and seek after open doors for development and advancement. By cultivating a development outlook, organizations can make a culture of versatility, flexibility, and persistent learning.

2. Empowering Input and Cycle: Input and emphasis are basic for driving improvement and advancement in business cycles, items, and administrations. Pioneers ought to urge representatives to give criticism, share thoughts, and take part in critical thinking and dynamic cycles. By requesting criticism and repeating on thoughts and arrangements, organizations can recognize regions for development, drive advancement, and remain in front of the opposition.

3. Executing Lean and Deft Practices: Lean and coordinated rehearses are important devices for driving nonstop improvement and transformation inside associations. Pioneers ought to take on lean standards, like waste decrease, process advancement, and nonstop improvement, to smooth out activities and increment productivity. Also, light-footed approaches, like Scrum or Kanban, can assist groups with adjusting rapidly to changing needs and convey worth to clients all the more really.

4. Estimating and Checking Execution: Estimating and observing execution is fundamental for driving ceaseless improvement and responsibility inside associations. Pioneers ought to lay out key execution markers (KPIs) and measurements that line up with vital targets and track progress toward objectives consistently. By observing execution and dissecting information, organizations can recognize patterns, potential open doors, and regions for development, driving constant improvement and advancement.

Developing accomplishment from inside associations requires an emphasis on guiding principle, culture, initiative turn of events, worker commitment, and persistent improvement. By putting resources into these inside factors, organizations can fabricate serious areas of strength for a for development, flexibility, and long haul progress in the present unique business climate.

Thus, as you endeavor to develop accomplishment from inside your association, make sure to focus on basic beliefs, cultivate a positive hierarchical culture, put resources into initiative turn of events, connect with workers, and drive persistent improvement. By zeroing in on these interior variables, you can make a flourishing and strong association that is strategically situated for outcome despite any test.

Chapter 6:

Creating a Lasting Impact in Your Business

In the steadily developing scene of business, making an enduring effect goes past momentary gains and benefits. It includes building a practical plan of action that drives monetary accomplishment as well as makes an incentive for partners, adds to the local area, and leaves a positive heritage for people in the future. In this complete aide, we will investigate procedures for making an enduring effect in your business, covering key regions, for example, reason driven administration, moral strategic policies, ecological supportability, social obligation, and development. By zeroing in on these center standards, organizations can fabricate a tradition of progress that stretches out a long ways past the primary concern.

Reason Driven Administration

1. Characterizing Your Motivation: Reason driven initiative starts with an unmistakable comprehension of your association's motivation - its justification behind presence past creating a gain. Pioneers ought to express a convincing vision and mission that mirrors the qualities, convictions, and yearnings of the association. By characterizing an unmistakable reason, pioneers can rouse workers, draw in clients, and separate their image in the commercial center.

2. Honest driving: Respectability is the underpinning of direction driven administration. Pioneers ought to maintain high moral guidelines, exhibit genuineness, straightforwardness, and responsibility in their activities, and focus on the interests of partners over transient additions. By driving with respectability, pioneers can construct trust, believability, and notoriety, laying the foundation for feasible achievement.

3. Engaging Others: Enabling others is fundamental for encouraging a culture of direction driven initiative. Pioneers ought to appoint authority, give independence, and backing workers in pursuing choices lined up with the association's motivation and values. By enabling others, pioneers can release the maximum capacity of their groups, drive advancement, and adjust all the more rapidly to change.

Moral Strategic approaches

1. Keeping up with Straightforwardness: Straightforwardness is fundamental for building trust and validity with partners. Organizations ought to be straightforward about their tasks, practices, and execution, revealing data transparently and genuinely to workers, clients, financial backers, and the general population. By keeping up with straightforwardness, organizations can exhibit respectability and responsibility, and cultivate trust and dedication among partners.

2. Maintaining Decency and Value: Reasonableness and value are crucial standards of moral strategic policies. Organizations ought to treat workers, clients, providers, and different partners with decency, regard, and poise, no matter what their experience, character, or status. By maintaining decency and value, organizations can establish a comprehensive and strong workplace, advance variety and incorporation, and improve notoriety and brand dependability.

3. Consistence and Legitimate Liability: Consistence with regulations, guidelines, and industry norms is fundamental for moral strategic policies. Organizations ought to lay out hearty consistence projects, approaches, and methodology to guarantee adherence to legitimate necessities and moral norms. By focusing on consistence and lawful obligation, organizations can relieve gambles, safeguard against liabilities, and keep up with respectability and dependability.

Natural Supportability

1. Diminishing Ecological Impression: Natural supportability includes limiting the ecological effect of business tasks and items. Organizations ought to take on reasonable practices and advancements to diminish energy utilization, squander age, and ozone depleting substance emanations. By carrying out energy-proficient cycles, reusing drives, and economical obtaining rehearses, organizations can diminish their natural impression and add to a better planet.

2. Monitoring Normal Assets: Saving regular assets is fundamental for safeguarding biodiversity and biological system wellbeing. Organizations ought to focus on asset protection and dependable asset the executives, like water protection, land safeguarding, and feasible ranger service rehearses. By moderating normal assets, organizations can limit natural debasement, support biological system benefits, and guarantee the accessibility of assets for people in the future.

3. Advancing Roundabout Economy: The round economy is a regenerative model that means to limit squander and expand asset productivity. Organizations ought to embrace the standards of the round economy by planning items for life span, reuse, and recyclability, and executing shut circle frameworks for asset recuperation and waste decrease. By advancing a roundabout economy, organizations can diminish dependence on limited assets, limit ecological effect, and make esteem from squander streams.

Social Obligation

1. Supporting People group Commitment: Social obligation includes supporting the networks in which organizations work through generosity, volunteerism, and local area commitment drives. Organizations ought to distinguish neighborhood necessities and amazing open doors for help, like schooling, medical services, or monetary turn of events, and contribute assets, skill, and time to address them. By supporting local area commitment, organizations can assemble altruism, upgrade notoriety, and reinforce associations with partners.

2. Advancing Variety and Consideration: Variety and incorporation are fundamental for encouraging a fair and impartial society. Organizations ought to focus on variety and consideration in their labor force, authority, and strategic approaches, and establish a comprehensive and strong workplace where all representatives feel esteemed and regarded. By advancing variety and consideration, organizations can take advantage of a more extensive ability pool, cultivate development, and improve inventiveness and cooperation.

3. Moral Store network The executives: Moral inventory network the board includes guaranteeing that providers and accomplices stick to moral principles and practices. Organizations ought to direct expected level of effort on providers, survey takes a chance with connected with work rehearses, basic liberties, and ecological effect, and lay out moral obtaining rules and principles. By advancing moral store network the executives, organizations can limit reputational gambles, guarantee consistence with legitimate and administrative prerequisites, and advance capable strategic policies all through the production network.

Advancement

1. Cultivating a Culture of Development: Advancement is fundamental for driving economical development and upper hand. Organizations ought to cultivate a culture of development that energizes innovativeness, trial and error, and chance taking, and rewards groundbreaking thoughts and leap forwards. By engaging representatives to enhance and investigate new open doors, organizations can drive persistent improvement, adjust to changing economic situations, and remain on the ball.

2. Putting resources into Innovative work: Innovative work (Research and development) are basic for driving development and mechanical progression. Organizations ought to put resources into Research and development drives that investigate new innovations, items, and administrations, and address developing business sector patterns and client needs. By putting resources into Research and development, organizations can separate their contributions, drive item advancement, and make an incentive for clients.

3. Teaming up for Development: Coordinated effort is fundamental for driving advancement and putting up novel thoughts for sale to the public. Organizations ought to team up with clients, providers, industry accomplices, scholastic establishments, and new businesses to share information, ability, and assets, and co-make imaginative arrangements. By encouraging joint effort, organizations can use assorted viewpoints, access new business sectors and advances, and speed up development and development.

Making an enduring effect in your business requires a comprehensive methodology that envelops reason driven initiative, moral strategic policies, ecological manageability, social obligation, and development. By zeroing in on these center standards, organizations can construct a supportable plan of action that drives monetary achievement, makes an incentive for partners, and leaves a positive heritage for people in the future.

In this way, as you endeavor to make an enduring effect in your business, make sure to lead with reason and honesty, focus on moral practices and ecological stewardship, support your local area and advance variety and consideration, and encourage a culture of development and joint effort. By embracing these standards, you can construct a strong and fruitful business that has a beneficial outcome on the planet.

Creating Your Special Counseling Personality

In the serious scene of counseling, laying out a special personality is fundamental for standing apart from the group, drawing in clients, and building an effective practice. Your counseling character envelops your image, values, ability, and way to deal with client administration, and separates you from different experts in your field. In this exhaustive aide, we will investigate procedures for making your extraordinary counseling character, covering key regions like characterizing your specialty, constructing your image, displaying your ability, and conveying outstanding worth to clients. By zeroing in on these center standards, you can separate yourself in the commercial center and position yourself for long haul achievement and development in the counseling business.

Characterizing Your Specialty

1. Recognizing Your Subject matters: The most vital phase in making your one of a kind counseling personality is to distinguish your specialized topics and specialization. Ponder your abilities, experience, and interests, and distinguish the regions where you succeed and have a profound comprehension. By zeroing in on your assets and ability, you can secure yourself as an expert in your specialty and draw in clients who esteem your extraordinary experiences and point of view.

2. Investigating Business sector Interest: Whenever you've recognized your subject matters, research market interest and distinguish open doors for specialization inside your specialty. Consider factors, for example, industry patterns, client needs, and serious scene, and distinguish regions where there is appeal for counseling administrations. By adjusting your specialty to showcase interest, you can situate yourself for progress and guarantee that there is a business opportunity for your administrations.

3. Characterizing Your Ideal interest group: Characterize your main interest group in view of your specialty and specialized topics. Recognize the kinds of clients you need to work with, for example, industry areas, organization sizes, or explicit difficulties they face. By understanding your ideal interest group and their requirements, you can tailor your administrations and informing to impact them and draw in the right clients to your training.

Building Your Image

1. **Fostering Your Image Personality:** Your image character envelops your visual components, informing, and generally impression you make with clients and possibilities. Foster a brand character that mirrors your qualities, character, and special selling suggestion. Think about components like your logo, variety range, typography, and manner of speaking, and guarantee consistency across the entirety of your advertising materials and correspondences.

2. **Making Convincing Informing:** Specialty convincing informing that imparts your offer and reverberates with your ideal interest group. Obviously eloquent what separates you from

different specialists in your specialty and how your administrations can address their particular requirements and difficulties. Use language that is clear, compact, and powerful, and feature your extraordinary assets, ability, and history of accomplishment.

3. Laying out Your Web-based Presence: Lay out areas of strength for a presence to feature your image and draw in clients. Make an expert site that features your administrations, skill, and client tributes, and gives important assets and content to your interest group. Utilize web-based entertainment stages like LinkedIn, Twitter, and Facebook to draw in with your crowd, share bits of knowledge and thought administration, and assemble associations with expected clients and industry powerhouses.

Exhibiting Your Mastery

1. Creating Thought Administration Content: Position yourself as an idea chief in your specialty by delivering excellent substance that shows your mastery and experiences. Compose blog entries, articles, whitepapers, or contextual analyses that address normal difficulties or patterns in your industry, and offer them with your crowd through your site, online entertainment, or email pamphlets. By giving important substance, you can lay out believability, draw in supporters, and fabricate entrust with expected clients.

2. Speaking Commitment and Studios: Talking commitment and studios are incredible open doors to feature your ability and interface with likely clients. Propose to talk at industry gatherings, occasions, or online classes, or host studios or instructional meetings on points applicable to your specialty. By offering your insight and experiences to a live crowd, you can show your skill, construct believability, and draw in new clients to your training.

3. Systems administration and Building Connections: Systems administration is fundamental for building your standing and extending your organization in the counseling business. Go to industry occasions, gatherings, or systems administration bunches where you can meet possible clients, colleagues, or reference accomplices. Fabricate associations with individual advisors, industry specialists, and thought pioneers, and search for amazing chances to team up or share references. By building areas of strength for an of gets in touch with, you can get to new open doors and extend your arrive at in the counseling local area.

Conveying Uncommon Worth to Clients

1. Understanding Client Needs: Find opportunity to figure out your clients' requirements, difficulties, and objectives prior to proposing arrangements. Lead careful exploration, pose testing inquiries, and listen effectively to their interests and targets. By acquiring a profound comprehension of your clients' necessities, you can fit your administrations and suggestions to address their particular prerequisites and convey greatest worth.

2. Giving Tweaked Arrangements: Offer altered arrangements that address your clients' extraordinary difficulties and targets. Stay away from one-size-fits-all methodologies and on second thought foster custom-made arrangements that line up with your clients' industry, culture, and objectives. By giving customized proposals and procedures, you can show your ability and obligation to conveying results that address your clients' issues and assumptions.

3. Estimating and Conveying Results: Measure and impart the consequences of your counseling commitment to show the worth you've conveyed to your clients. Utilize key execution markers (KPIs), measurements, or benchmarks to follow progress and results, and offer standard updates with your clients on the effect of your work. By showing substantial outcomes and profit from speculation, you can construct trust, validity, and dependability with your clients and support rehash business and references.

Making your interesting counseling personality requires an essential methodology that incorporates characterizing your specialty, fabricating your image, exhibiting your skill, and conveying uncommon worth to clients. By zeroing in on these center standards and techniques, you can separate yourself in the commercial center, draw in clients who esteem your one of a kind viewpoint and skill, and fabricate a fruitful counseling practice that goes the distance.

Along these lines, as you set out on your excursion to make your extraordinary counseling character, make sure to characterize your specialty, fabricate your image, grandstand your skill, and convey excellent worth to your clients. By zeroing in on these key regions, you can secure yourself as a confided in guide, thought pioneer, and go-to master in your field, and make an enduring effect in the counseling business.

Developing a Prosperous Demeanor

In the dynamic and serious universe of business, disposition assumes a significant part in deciding achievement. A prosperous mentality envelops idealism, strength, inventiveness, and a development outlook, and is fundamental for conquering difficulties, quickly jumping all over chances, and accomplishing long haul flourishing. In this extensive aide, we will investigate procedures for developing a prosperous mentality in the business space, covering key regions like outlook, strength, versatility, and energy. By zeroing in on these center standards, people can foster the attitude and propensities expected to flourish in the present quickly changing business scene and open their maximum capacity for progress.

Grasping the Force of Mentality

1. Fostering a Development Outlook: A development mentality is the conviction that capacities and knowledge can be created through commitment and difficult work. People with a development mentality embrace difficulties, gain from disappointments, and persevere despite misfortunes. To develop a prosperous mentality, it's fundamental to embrace a development outlook and view snags as any open doors for development and advancing as opposed to impossible boundaries.

2. Rehearsing Positive Self-Talk: Positive self-talk includes supplanting negative considerations and convictions with positive attestations and support. By deliberately reexamining negative contemplations into positive ones, people can develop a more hopeful and enabled mentality. Rehearsing positive self-talk can help certainty, inspiration, and versatility, empowering people to defeat hindrances and accomplish their objectives.

3. Imagining Achievement: Perception is a strong strategy for programming the brain for progress. By picturing themselves accomplishing their objectives and encountering outcome in clear detail, people can fortify their faith in their capacities and increment their inspiration and assurance. Normal perception activities can assist people with remaining on track, motivated, and focused on their objectives, even despite difficulties or mishaps.

Building Versatility

1. Embracing Disappointment as a Learning An open door: Disappointment is an unavoidable piece of the excursion to progress. Rather than review disappointment as a misfortune, people ought to embrace it as an important learning a valuable open door. By examining disappointments, distinguishing examples learned, and applying them to future undertakings, people can develop further and stronger over the long haul.

2. Developing Capacity to appreciate individuals on a deeper level: The ability to appreciate people on a deeper level is the capacity to perceive, comprehend, and deal with one's own feelings and those of others. People with high capacity to understand individuals on a profound level are better outfitted to adapt to pressure, explore difficulties, and keep an uplifting outlook notwithstanding misfortune. By developing ability to understand people on a deeper level through mindfulness, sympathy, and compelling correspondence, people can improve their versatility and flexibility in the business space.

3. Rehearsing Care: Care includes focusing on the current second with transparency, interest, and acknowledgment. By rehearsing care contemplation or care based procedures, people can diminish pressure, increment mindfulness, and develop a feeling of quiet and clearness. Care can assist people with building flexibility by empowering them to remain on track, formed, and creative, even in testing circumstances.

Embracing Flexibility

1. Staying Adaptable Even with Change: Versatility is the capacity to acclimate to new conditions and explore change actually. In the present quickly developing business climate, flexibility is fundamental for remaining serious and taking advantage of chances. People ought to embrace change as a characteristic piece of the business scene and stay adaptable and receptive in their way to deal with critical thinking and navigation.

2. Looking for Open doors for Development and Advancement: Change frequently presents valuable open doors for development and advancement. Rather than opposing change, people ought to effectively search out chances to enhance and work on existing cycles, items, or administrations. By embracing change as an impetus for development, people can remain on the ball and position themselves for long haul outcome in the business space.

3. Building a Different Range of abilities: In a quickly changing business climate, people ought to persistently try to grow and expand their range of abilities. By gaining new abilities, information, and skills, people can adjust to developing business sector requests, influence arising innovations, and benefit from new open doors for development and headway. Building a different range of abilities improves people's versatility and strength, empowering them to flourish in an assortment of business settings.

Encouraging Energy

1. Rehearsing Appreciation: Appreciation is the act of communicating appreciation for the endowments and open doors in one's day to day existence. By developing an outlook of appreciation and zeroing in on the positive parts of life and work, people can move their viewpoint from shortage to overflow. Rehearsing appreciation can increment satisfaction, lessen pressure, and work on by and large prosperity, cultivating a more sure and prosperous mentality in the business space.

2. Encircling Yourself with Energy: individuals we encircle ourselves with fundamentally affect our perspectives and point of view. People ought to search out certain, steady, and similar people who motivate and urge them to arrive at their maximum capacity. By encircling themselves with energy, people can develop a steady organization of friends, tutors, and partners who elevate and engage them on their excursion to progress.

3 Observing Triumphs, Of all shapes and sizes: Commending victories, regardless of how little, is fundamental for keeping up with inspiration, spirit, and energy. People ought to find opportunity to recognize and commend their accomplishments, achievements, and progress toward their objectives. By praising victories, people can support positive ways of behaving, fabricate certainty, and support their inspiration and obligation to progress in the business area.

Developing a prosperous demeanor is fundamental for outcome in the business space. By fostering a development mentality, building strength, embracing versatility, and encouraging energy, people can beat difficulties, immediately jump all over chances, and accomplish their objectives in the present dynamic and cutthroat business scene.

Thus, as you leave on your excursion to develop a prosperous mentality, make sure to take on a development outlook, fabricate flexibility, embrace versatility, and cultivate energy in all parts of your life and work. By zeroing in on these center standards and techniques, you can open your maximum capacity and make long haul progress and flourishing in the business space.

Chapter 7:

Mastering the Art of Negotiation

Exchange is a major expertise in the business world, fundamental for accomplishing positive results, settling clashes, and building effective organizations. Whether arranging bargains, agreements, pay rates, or settling questions, excelling at exchange can give people an upper hand and improve their viability as business experts. In this complete aide, we will investigate methodologies for excelling at exchange, covering key regions, for example, readiness, correspondence, critical thinking, and relationship building. By leveling up these fundamental abilities, people can turn out to be more certain, powerful moderators and accomplish ideal outcomes in their business tries.

Grasping the Basics of Exchange

1. Characterizing Discussion: Exchange is a course of correspondence and split the difference wherein parties with clashing interests look to agree. It includes the trading of offers, counteroffers, and concessions, fully intent on accomplishing a good result for all gatherings included. Powerful discussion requires undivided attention, influential correspondence, critical thinking, and relationship building abilities.

2. Recognizing Key Components: Discussion includes a few key components, including interests, choices, choices, and positions. Interests are the basic necessities, wants, and concerns driving each party's way of behaving and choices. Choices are the accessible choices or options in contrast to agreeing assuming that discussions fizzle. Choices are expected arrangements or recommendations that meet the interests of the two players. Positions are explicit requests, offers, or proposition set forth by each party during dealings.

3. Perceiving Different Discussion Styles: Arbitrators might embrace different exchange styles in light of their characters, inclinations, and social foundations. Normal discussion styles incorporate cutthroat, cooperative, obliging, and splitting the difference. Cutthroat mediators focus on their own advantages and look to augment their benefits, frequently to the detriment of the other party. Cooperative arbitrators center around tracking down commonly advantageous arrangements and building trust and affinity with the other party. Obliging mediators focus on keeping up with connections and fulfilling the other party's requirements, now and again to the detriment of their own. Compromising moderators look to track down center ground and make concessions to arrive at a commonly satisfactory understanding.

Planning for Exchange

1. Laying out Targets and Objectives: Prior to entering dealings, it's fundamental to explain your targets, objectives, and wanted results. Recognize your inclinations, needs, and non-negotiables, and lay out clear benchmarks for progress. Decide your best option in contrast to an arranged understanding (BATNA) and reservation point, or the base OK result you will acknowledge. Putting forth targets and objectives helps center your endeavors, guide your technique, and measure your progress in dealings.

2. Leading Exploration and Investigation: Planning is critical to fruitful exchange. Lead exhaustive examination and investigation on the other party, their inclinations, needs, and expected other options. Assemble data on economic situations, industry guidelines, and important lawful or administrative issues. Examine the qualities, shortcomings, open doors, and dangers (SWOT investigation) of your situation and the other party's situation. By outfitting yourself with information and data, you can expect difficulties, recognize open doors, and foster viable discussion systems.

3. Fostering an Exchange System: In light of your targets, objectives, and examination, foster a discussion procedure that frames your methodology, strategies, and key messages. Consider factors like timing, sequencing, and outlining of proposition. Expect likely complaints, concessions, and counteroffers from the other party, and get ready reactions and counterarguments. Decide your initial proposition, target result, and backup positions, and be ready to adjust your procedure in view of advancements during discussions.

Powerful Correspondence in Exchange

1. Undivided attention: Undivided attention is a basic correspondence expertise in exchange. Center around grasping the other party's inclinations, concerns, and viewpoints, and listen mindfully to their verbal and non-verbal signs. Pose explaining inquiries, rework their assertions, and reflect back their feelings to show sympathy and understanding. By rehearsing undivided attention, you can assemble compatibility, lay out trust, and reveal open doors for joint effort and split the difference.

2. Clear and Succinct Correspondence: Clear and brief correspondence is fundamental for passing on your message successfully and keeping away from mistaken assumptions or misinterpretations. Utilize basic, clear language, and keep away from language or specialized terms that might confound or estrange the other party. Obviously lucid your inclinations, needs, and proposition, and give supporting proof or reasoning to legitimize your positions. Be ready to make sense of complicated ideas or issues in a manner that is open and reasonable to the next party.

3 Decisiveness and Influence: Confidence is the capacity to communicate your necessities, interests, and limits unhesitatingly and consciously. In discussion, self-assuredness is fundamental for upholding for your inclinations, safeguarding your positions, and declaring your freedoms. Utilize self-assured language, tone, and non-verbal communication to convey certainty and conviction in your recommendations. Influence includes affecting the other party's mentalities, convictions, and ways of behaving through compelling correspondence methods, for example, narrating, outlining, and social evidence. By excelling at influence, you can convince the other party to acknowledge your recommendations and arrive at a commonly valuable understanding.

Critical thinking and Inventiveness

1. Cooperative Critical thinking: Cooperative critical thinking includes cooperating with the other party to distinguish and address shared difficulties or valuable open doors. Move toward exchanges as a critical thinking exercise as opposed to a lose situation, and spotlight on making esteem and boosting joint increases. Conceptualize intelligent fixes, investigate compromises, and search for shared benefit results that fulfill the two players' inclinations.

By encouraging a feeling of coordinated effort and participation, you can fabricate trust and compatibility with the other party and improve the probability of arriving at a commonly useful understanding.

2. Producing Choices and Choices: Producing choices and options is fundamental for growing the pie and making esteem in talks. Conceptualize numerous arrangements or proposition that address the two players' inclinations and needs, and consider innovative or offbeat ways to deal with critical thinking. Investigate different compromises, complete bundles, or prospective arrangements that address the issues of the two players. By producing a different scope of choices and options, you can increment adaptability, upgrade imagination, and defeat stalemates in talks.

3. Adjusting and Adaptability: Discussion is a dynamic and liquid interaction that requires versatility and adaptability. Be ready to adjust your system, strategies, and recommendations in view of advancements during dealings. Stay open to new data, input, and points of view from the other party, and change your positions or make concessions if vital. By showing adaptability and eagerness to think twice about, can construct trust, work with understanding, and accomplish fruitful results in exchanges.

Constructing and Keeping up with Connections

1. Laying out Compatibility and Trust: Building affinity and trust is fundamental for laying out sure and useful connections in discussions. Figure out some shared interest with the other party, show compassion and understanding, and impart straightforwardly and straightforwardly. Tell the truth, solid, and reliable in your communications, and completely finish your responsibilities and commitments. By building compatibility and trust, you can make an establishment for coordinated effort, participation, and common regard in dealings.

2. Dealing with Feelings and Struggle: Feelings and struggle are unavoidable in discussions, yet what you oversee them can mean for the result. Remain even headed, formed, and centered under tension, and abstain from responding rashly or genuinely to incitements or conflicts. Utilize the capacity to appreciate anyone on a deeper level abilities like mindfulness, self-guideline, and sympathy to deal with your own feelings and grasp the other party's point of view. At the point when clashes emerge, center around finding useful arrangements and de-heightening pressures to save the uprightness of the exchange cycle.

3 Haggling with Honesty and Morals: Uprightness and morals are basic standards in discussion. Continuously haggle with genuineness, uprightness, and reasonableness, and stick to moral guidelines and lawful commitments. Stay away from misleading or manipulative strategies, for example, feigning, misrepresenting, or covering data, as they can subvert trust and harm associations with the other party. Haggle with sincere intentions, regard the other party's inclinations and limits, and endeavor to accomplish results that are commonly advantageous and morally sound.

Becoming amazing at discussion is fundamental for outcome in the business field. By understanding the essentials of exchange, planning actually, imparting powerfully, critical thinking imaginatively, and building solid connections, people can turn out to be more certain, compelling moderators and accomplish ideal results in their business tries.

Thus, as you endeavor to excel at discussion, make sure to set clear targets, direct careful readiness, convey actually, center around critical thinking and innovativeness, and construct and keep up with positive associations with the other party. By leveling up these fundamental abilities and methodologies, you can turn into a more fruitful and persuasive moderator and accomplish your objectives in the cutthroat universe of business.

Laying down a good foundation for Yourself as a Chief Specialist

In the present quickly developing business scene, specialists assume an essential part in assisting associations with exploring complex difficulties, drive development, and accomplish their essential targets. As the interest for specific mastery and key direction keeps on developing, securing yourself as a chief specialist can furnish you with a strategic advantage and open up new open doors for development and headway. In this far reaching guide, we will investigate systems for laying down a good foundation for yourself as a head specialist, covering key regions like structure skill, developing validity, supporting connections, and conveying uncommon worth to clients. By executing these methodologies, you can situate yourself as a confided in counselor and go-to master in your field, and fabricate a fruitful counseling practice that flourishes in the present cutthroat business climate.

Building Aptitude and Specialization

1. Recognizing Your Specialty: The most important phase in securing yourself as a head expert is to distinguish your specialty or area of specialization. Ponder your abilities, experience, and interests, and recognize the regions where you have the most aptitude and information. Consider factors, for example, industry patterns, market interest, and your special incentive, and pick a specialty that lines up with your assets and interests. By zeroing in on a particular specialty, you can separate yourself from contenders and position yourself as a specialist in your field.

2. Proceeding with Training and Expert Turn of events: Constant learning is fundamental for remaining pertinent and cutthroat in the counseling business. Put resources into progressing training and expert improvement valuable chances to extend your mastery, grow your range of abilities, and keep up to date with arising patterns and advances in your field. Go to industry gatherings, studios, and preparing programs, seek after accreditations or postgraduate educations, and search out mentorship or instructing from old pros. By putting resources into your expert turn of events, you can upgrade your validity and capability as a specialist and offer more noteworthy benefit to your clients.

3. Building an Arrangement of Progress: Building an arrangement of fruitful tasks and client commitment is fundamental for laying out validity and showing your skill as a specialist. Exhibit your previous work, accomplishments, and results in a portfolio or contextual investigations that feature your commitments and effect on clients' organizations. Utilize substantial models, measurements, and tributes to delineate your abilities and history of progress. By building serious areas of strength for a, you can construct entrust with likely clients and separate yourself as a chief specialist in your specialty.

Developing Believability and Trust

1. Showing Thought Authority: Thought authority is a strong method for laying out believability and perceivability in your field. Share your bits of knowledge, mastery, and points of view on industry patterns, best practices, and arising issues through articles, blog entries, whitepapers, or talking commitment. Distribute content on your site, web-based entertainment stages, or industry distributions, and position yourself as a confided in wellspring of data and mastery in your specialty. By showing figured administration, you can draw in clients, construct your standing, and secure yourself as a main expert in your field.

2. Looking for Supports and Tributes: Client tributes and supports are significant resources for building believability and trust as an expert. Urge fulfilled clients to give tributes or supports of your work, and grandstand them conspicuously on your site, advertising materials, or LinkedIn profile. Client tributes act as friendly verification of your mastery and viability as a specialist, and can assist with consoling imminent clients of the quality and worth of your administrations. By gathering and displaying tributes, you can fortify your standing and validity as a head expert.

3. Systems administration and Relationship Building: Systems administration and relationship building are fundamental for setting up a good foundation for yourself as a head specialist and growing your client base. Go to industry occasions, gatherings, or systems administration bunches where you can meet likely clients, colleagues, or reference accomplices. Fabricate associations with individual specialists, industry specialists, and thought innovators in your specialty, and search for potential chances to team up or share references. By building areas of strength for an of contacts and connections, you can get to new open doors, extend your span, and fabricate believability and entrust with expected clients.

Conveying Extraordinary Worth to Clients

1. Understanding Client Needs and Goals: To secure yourself as a head specialist, it's fundamental to figure out your clients' necessities, targets, and difficulties. Find opportunity to stand by listening to your clients, pose testing inquiries, and direct intensive evaluations of their business objectives and necessities. By acquiring a profound comprehension of your clients' requirements, you can fit your answers and suggestions to really address their particular difficulties and targets.

2. Giving Key Direction and Arrangements: As a head specialist, your job is to give key direction and arrangements that assist clients with accomplishing their business goals. Offer bits of knowledge, ability, and counsel that go past the surface level and offer certified benefit to your clients. Foster modified methodologies, plans, or suggestions that line up with your clients' objectives and needs, and assist them with defeating impediments and benefit from open doors. By giving vital direction and arrangements, you can show your aptitude and obligation to conveying results that drive substantial business results for your clients.

3. Estimating and Exhibiting Results: Estimating and showing the aftereffects of your counseling commitment is fundamental for laying out believability and demonstrating the worth of your administrations to clients. Characterize clear targets, measurements, and key execution pointers (KPIs) for each undertaking or commitment, and track progress and results against these benchmarks. Discuss consistently with your clients, give refreshes on project achievements and accomplishments, and offer reports or introductions that feature the effect of your work. By estimating and showing results, you can construct trust, validity, and certainty with your clients and position yourself as a head expert who conveys quantifiable worth.

Adjusting to Developing Business sector Patterns

1. Remaining Spry and Adaptable: The counseling business is continually advancing, with new innovations, patterns, and market elements forming client needs and assumptions. To set up a good foundation for yourself as a head specialist, remaining spry and adaptable in your way to deal with serving clients is fundamental. Stay up to date with arising patterns, advances, and best practices in your field, and adjust your administrations and contributions to satisfy developing client needs. By remaining deft and adaptable, you can expect changes on the lookout and position yourself as a believed guide who gives imaginative arrangements and bits of knowledge to clients.

2. Embracing Advancement and Imagination: Development and innovativeness are key drivers of outcome in the counseling business. As a chief specialist, search out chances to improve and separate yourself from contenders by offering extraordinary arrangements, approaches, or procedures. Energize imagination and cooperation inside your group, and investigate better approaches to enhance clients' organizations through inventive reasoning and critical thinking. By embracing development and innovativeness, you can remain on the ball and position yourself as a ground breaking expert who conveys state of the art answers for clients.

3. Putting resources into Innovation and Apparatuses: Innovation assumes an undeniably significant part in the counseling business, empowering specialists to convey more productive, viable, and effective answers for clients. Put resources into innovation and devices that improve your abilities and smooth out your tasks, for example, project the executives programming, information investigation instruments, or cooperation stages. Influence innovation to robotize routine errands, assemble bits of knowledge from information, and speak with clients all the more actually. By putting resources into innovation and instruments, you can work on your proficiency, efficiency, and seriousness as an expert, and convey more noteworthy worth to your clients.

Setting up a good foundation for yourself as a chief specialist requires an essential methodology that envelops building mastery, developing believability, conveying extraordinary worth to clients, and adjusting to developing business sector patterns. By zeroing in on these center standards and techniques, you can separate yourself in the cutthroat counseling scene, draw in clients who esteem your skill and bits of knowledge, and construct a fruitful counseling practice that flourishes in the present unique business climate.

Thus, as you leave on your excursion to lay down a good foundation for yourself as a chief specialist, make sure to fabricate mastery in your specialty, develop validity and entrust with clients, convey excellent worth through essential direction and arrangements, and adjust to developing business sector patterns with readiness and advancement. By following these procedures, you can situate yourself as a confided in counselor and go-to master in your field, and fabricate an effective counseling practice that conveys quantifiable worth to clients.

Arranging Your Direction to Abundance

Discussion is a principal expertise in the realm of business. Whether you're shutting bargains, getting associations, or exploring clashes, your capacity to haggle really can fundamentally affect your prosperity and monetary prosperity. In this exhaustive aide, we will investigate the systems, strategies, and mentality expected to arrange your direction to abundance in the business community. From arrangement and correspondence to critical thinking and relationship-building, excelling at exchange can open doors, boost worth, and drive monetary progress in your business tries.

Grasping the Force of Exchange

1. Characterizing Exchange: Discussion is a course of correspondence and split the difference where parties with clashing interests try to agree. It includes the trading of offers, counteroffers, and concessions, fully intent on accomplishing a good result for all gatherings included. Compelling discussion requires a blend of logical abilities, the capacity to understand individuals on a profound level, and vital reasoning.

2. Perceiving the Significance of Exchange in Business: Discussion is a basic expertise in the realm of business, where each exchange, organization, or understanding includes some level of discussion. Whether you're arranging agreements, compensations, or agreements, your capacity to haggle actually can affect your main concern and decide your outcome in the commercial center. By excelling at exchange, you can open doors, augment esteem, and accomplish your monetary objectives in business.

3. Grasping the Elements of Exchange: Discussion is a dynamic and liquid interaction that requires versatility, innovativeness, and flexibility. It includes figuring out the interests, needs, and inspirations of the two players, and settling on something worth agreeing on and commonly valuable arrangements. Exchange is definitely not a lose situation where one party wins and the other loses, yet rather a cooperative work to make esteem and accomplish shared goals.

Planning for Discussion

1. Putting forth Targets and Objectives: Prior to going into talks, it's fundamental to explain your targets, objectives, and wanted results. What do you expect to accomplish through the discussion cycle? What are your needs and non-negotiables? By laying out clear targets and objectives, you can concentrate your endeavors, guide your procedure, and measure your progress in discussions.

2. Directing Exploration and Examination: Readiness is critical to effective exchange. Direct careful examination and investigation on the other party, their inclinations, needs, and expected other options. Accumulate data on economic situations, industry guidelines, and applicable lawful or administrative issues. Dissect the qualities, shortcomings, open doors, and dangers (SWOT investigation) of your situation and the other party's situation. By furnishing yourself with information and data, you can expect difficulties, recognize potential open doors, and foster viable exchange systems.

3. Fostering a Discussion Methodology: In view of your targets, objectives, and exploration, foster an exchange system that frames your methodology, strategies, and key messages. Consider factors like timing, sequencing, and outlining of recommendations. Expect possible protests, concessions, and counteroffers from the other party, and get ready reactions and counterarguments. Decide your initial proposition, target result, and backup positions, and be ready to adjust your system in light of advancements during talks.

Powerful Correspondence in Exchange

1. Undivided attention: Undivided attention is a basic correspondence expertise in exchange. Center around grasping the other party's inclinations, concerns, and viewpoints, and listen mindfully to their verbal and non-verbal signals. Pose explaining inquiries, rework their assertions, and reflect back their feelings to show compassion and understanding. By rehearsing undivided attention, you can fabricate affinity, lay out trust, and reveal open doors for cooperation and split the difference.

2. Clear and Succinct Correspondence: Clear and compact correspondence is fundamental for passing on your message really and keeping away from errors or misinterpretations. Utilize basic, clear language, and keep away from language or specialized terms that might confound or distance the other party. Obviously lucid your inclinations, needs, and recommendations, and give supporting proof or reasoning to legitimize your positions. Be ready to make sense of perplexing ideas or issues in a manner that is open and reasonable to the next party.

3. Emphaticness and Influence: Decisiveness is the capacity to communicate your necessities, interests, and limits with certainty and consciously. In exchange, emphaticness is fundamental for upholding for your inclinations, guarding your positions, and affirming your privileges. Utilize confident language, tone, and non-verbal communication to convey certainty and conviction in your recommendations. Influence includes impacting the other party's mentalities, convictions, and ways of behaving through successful correspondence procedures, for example, narrating, outlining, and social evidence. By excelling at influence, you can convince the other party to acknowledge your recommendations and arrive at a commonly helpful understanding.

Critical thinking and Imagination

1. Cooperative Critical thinking: Cooperative critical thinking includes cooperating with the other party to distinguish and address shared difficulties or open doors. Move toward exchanges as a critical thinking exercise instead of a lose situation, and spotlight on making esteem and expanding joint increases. Conceptualize savvy fixes, investigate compromises, and search for mutual benefit results that fulfill the two players' inclinations. By cultivating a feeling of joint effort and participation, you can construct trust and compatibility with the other party and improve the probability of arriving at a commonly helpful understanding.

2. Producing Choices and Options: Producing choices and options is fundamental for growing the pie and making esteem in dealings. Conceptualize different arrangements or proposition that address the two players' inclinations and needs, and consider imaginative or offbeat ways to deal with critical thinking. Investigate different compromises, all inclusive bundles, or proposed arrangements that address the issues of the two players. By producing a different scope of choices and options, you can increment adaptability, upgrade imagination, and defeat stalemates in discussions.

3. Versatility and Adaptability: Discussion is a dynamic and liquid cycle that requires flexibility and adaptability. Be ready to adjust your technique, strategies, and recommendations in view of improvements during talks. Stay open to new data, criticism, and points of view from the other party, and change your positions or make concessions if fundamental. By showing adaptability and readiness to think twice about, can fabricate trust, work with understanding, and accomplish effective results in talks.

Assembling and Keeping up with Connections

1. Laying out Compatibility and Trust: Building affinity and trust is fundamental for laying out sure and useful connections in talks. Settle on something worth agreeing on with the other party, exhibit sympathy and understanding, and impart straightforwardly and straightforwardly. Tell the truth, dependable, and predictable in your cooperations, and finish your responsibilities and commitments. By building compatibility and trust, you can make an establishment for joint effort, participation, and common regard in exchanges.

2. Dealing with Feelings and Struggle: Feelings and struggle are unavoidable in exchanges, yet what you oversee them can mean for the result. Keep mentally collected, created, and centered under tension, and abstain from responding indiscreetly or sincerely to incitements or conflicts. Utilize the ability to appreciate anyone on a profound level abilities like mindfulness, self-guideline, and sympathy to deal with your own feelings and grasp the other party's viewpoint. At the point when clashes emerge, center around finding productive arrangements and de-raising pressures to safeguard the honesty of the exchange cycle.

3. Haggling with Respectability and Morals: Honesty and morals are crucial standards in discussion. Continuously haggle with trustworthiness, respectability, and reasonableness, and stick to moral principles and legitimate commitments. Stay away from tricky or manipulative strategies, for example, feigning, overstating, or covering data, as they can sabotage trust and harm associations with the other party. Haggle with honest intentions, regard the other party's inclinations and limits, and endeavor to accomplish results that are commonly valuable and morally sound.

Exchange is an integral asset for making riches and progress in the business community. By excelling at exchange and executing systems for successful correspondence, critical thinking, and relationship-building, you can open doors, amplify esteem, and accomplish your monetary objectives in business. In this way, as you arrange your direction to riches, make sure to set clear targets, get ready completely, impart successfully, and construct trust and compatibility with the other party. By following these standards and methodologies, you can haggle with certainty and accomplish ideal results in your business tries.

Conclusion:

Flourishing in Your Wealth Garden

As we finish up our excursion through the craft of exchange and its significant effect on business achievement, obviously dominating this expertise is similar to watching out for a thriving nursery of riches. Similarly as a gifted landscaper supports each plant with care and consideration, so too should we develop our discussion capacities to yield plentiful compensations in the business field.

In the nursery of exchange, planning fills in as the rich soil from which achievement blooms. Laying out clear targets and objectives sows the seeds of goal, while examination and investigation give the supplements expected to development. With a very much tended establishment, we can explore the exciting bends in the road of discussion with certainty and balance.

Compelling correspondence goes about as the daylight that enlightens our way, illuminating open doors and enlightening the way forward. Through undivided attention, clear enunciation, and influential exchange, we can cultivate understanding and coordinated effort, sustaining connections that prove to be fruitful for quite a long time into the future.

Critical thinking and imagination act as the water that supports our nursery, extinguishing the thirst of contention and sustaining the seeds of advancement. By embracing cooperation, producing choices, and adjusting to change, we can beat difficulties and develop arrangements that twist in even the most bone-dry of conditions.

Relationship-building is the rich ground from which enduring success comes out. By laying out affinity and trust, dealing with feelings and struggle, and haggling with uprightness and morals, we can plant the seeds of organization and common regard, receiving the benefits of productive joint effort and shared achievement.

As we keep an eye on our abundance garden with industriousness and care, we embrace a prosperous future loaded up with an open door and overflow. By leveling up our discussion abilities and applying them with shrewdness and premonition, we can explore the always changing scene of business with certainty and beauty, thriving in the nursery through our own effort.

In this way, as you leave on your excursion to develop your way to success, make sure to keep an eye on your abundance garden with goal and reason, sustaining every discussion with care and consideration. By embracing the standards of powerful correspondence, critical thinking, and relationship-building, you can develop a future loaded up with progress, overflow, and satisfaction.

Consulting Gold

220